Praise for *Your Best Work*...

"*Your Best Work* is the modern guide to meaningful work. Tom Morin understands the nuances of modern work and what it takes to truly do your best work today, tomorrow, and every day."

ERIC TERMUENDE, leading public speaker and bestselling author of *Rethink Work*

"Tom Morin connects the work we do with the difference it makes. Your work and your company can make the world a better place, and *Your Best Work* shows how."

PAUL KRISMER, international employee engagement speaker and bestselling author of *Whole Person Happiness*

"*Your Best Work* offers a pragmatic and structured approach to discover our way to meaningful work. Tom Morin distills the process into simple and actionable steps to propel individuals and organizations forward into a new world of work."

ERNEST BARBARIC, executive coach and host of *Art of Meaningful Work*

"Tom Morin enables you to envision the work that is meaningful to you and gives you a road map to get there. In *Your Best Work*, Morin uses real-life examples to inspire and empower readers to create change in their working lives."

TRACY GUILLET, therapist to the more introverted and keynote speaker

"It's unusual in a business book to be 'gripped,' but I was taken in from the beginning of Tom Morin's extremely well-written book. Morin writes beautifully about our search for meaning at work, and our desire to take control of our working lives. He presents a level-headed and easy to understand model that's valuable for anyone setting out in their career, or looking to reassess it. I wish I had this book when I started out. An excellent read."

CHRIS HOOD, Director of Consulting at Advanced Workplace Associates

"At some point we will all ask ourselves two questions: 'What am I here to do?' and 'How can I be my best?' Most days we will avert our gaze and turn away from these transformational questions. When you tire of that strategy, and are drawn to discover your own answers, you will find indispensable guidance in the ideas, insights, and examples Tom Morin has included in this approachable, engaging, and very well-written book."

SCOTT RICHARDSON, Master Certified Coach (MCC) and Director of Training, Royal Roads University Graduate Certificate in Executive Coaching

**YOUR
BEST
WORK**

Steve,

How you do
your work
contributes to my
well-being.

Thank you,
Tom.

Create the Working Life
That's Right for You

Your
Best
Work

TOM MORIN

PAGE TWO
BOOKS

Cataloguing in publication information is available from
Library and Archives Canada.

ISBN 978-1-989603-50-5 (print)
ISBN 978-1-989603-51-2 (ebook)

Some names and identifying details have been changed
to protect the privacy of individuals.

This publication is meant to be a source of accurate information for the
reader in regard to the subject matter covered. It is not meant as a sub-
stitute for direct, expert assistance. If such assistance is required, then
the services of a competent professional should be sought.

Page Two
www.pagetwo.com

Edited by Amanda Lewis
Copyedited by John Sweet
Cover design by Emanuel Ilagan
Interior design by Fiona Lee

workfeelsgood.com

To Joanna,
for her unwavering support and love

Contents

"What you get
is a living—
what you give
is a life."

LILLIAN GISH

Author's Note

W E CRAVE MEANINGFUL work. We want to make a difference through our work. But making our jobs meaningful, or finding new meaningful work, is one of the most difficult things we'll ever do.

In this book, I describe the barriers to meaningful work and how to overcome them. My approach is an outcome of facing challenges, and sometimes danger, in my own working life, and my experience as a consultant to organizations and coach to individuals.

1

Dying for Work

Y FIRST JOB as an adult was in the military. I was an army electronics technician, but like everyone in the army, I was trained to be a soldier first. My training protected me many times, and on one day it saved my life.

In 1993 I was deployed to what was then called the former Yugoslavia. Beginning in 1991 and lasting until 2001, there was a series of ethnically based wars and insurgencies now known as the Yugoslav Wars. I was attached to the maintenance platoon of the Princess Patricia's Canadian Light Infantry (PPCLI). We were part of the United Nations Protection Force and our role was to maintain peace in established safe zones and control borders.

The soldiers of the PPCLI are a professional, highly skilled, and well-equipped fighting force. In September 1993 in the

Medak Pocket in southern Croatia, they drove off an assault in what was, at that time, the most severe battle fought by Canadians since the Korean War. But while the infantry was taking heavy shelling in Medak and coming close to running out of ammunition, I was behind the front lines in our maintenance compound.

Only a few other jobs might be like being a soldier—for example, a police officer. Jobs that require sacrificing our life in service to our country and community are often regarded as some of the most noble and meaningful careers we can have.

But being in the military was difficult for me. Although I always received great performance reviews, I never liked being an electronics technician. I found the work unfulfilling, and the rigid military discipline made me miserable. Before that deployment in 1993, I was often immersed in my hobbies to distract myself from the day-to-day boredom of my job. I spent a lot of time hiking and camping in the local wilderness. I spent a lot of money on cars. I played guitar, and I actually quit the military for nine months to try to make it as a musician. When my money ran out, the military took me back.

When they took me back, I was reassigned to a base in a different city and I arrived a day before and got a hotel room. I was supposed to be at the base the next morning to be issued uniforms and an identification card. But that night in my hotel room, as I sat hunched on the edge of the bed, I had one of my darkest moments. My long musician's hair had been cut a few days earlier. I was in a city where I knew no one and I was going to a strange workplace to do a job that I had found so unfulfilling. I cried for about an hour and I don't remember if I slept that night.

In the morning, I drove to the base. Just before the guard-house, I stopped on the side of the road and thought about turning around. But where would I go? What would I do? My father had been in the military for twenty-four years. I had joined right out of high school. It was the only real job I had ever had. Instead of turning my car around, I decided to dedicate myself to being the best soldier and technician I could be.

Those first few months were tough. The following years were better. I was given extensive training on state-of-the-art equipment and I was promoted into my first leadership role. I was trained for war and I was going to a war zone, the former Yugoslavia. I was trained to want just that. My home unit was sending one of their best technicians, and my next promotion would be waiting for me when I returned.

The deployment was everything I wanted it to be. It had intensity, learning, camaraderie, and adventure. One time, we were set up in a large, open field for a couple of weeks as we travelled to a new sector. The warring factions had bombed the nearby towns into rubble. There were very few people still living in the area and those who were had nothing left. Family members were dead. Most of the water wells were poisoned; livestock had been killed and crops burned.

One day, an elderly woman came by my truck. She stood far enough away to show she knew to keep her distance from our supplies and equipment. She smiled and I said hello, one of the few things I could say in Croatian. I gestured for her to sit on an empty wire roll that I was using as a chair. She sat staring out into the field and looking as though she needed a safe place to rest. I offered her some food. It was a ration pack of ground beef in tomato sauce. She ate, sat for a short while, then left. After that, she came by most days and always smiled, sat quietly, and left right after she finished eating. We soon left that place and I never saw her again. I had a lot of deeply meaningful experiences like that. I loved that deployment right up until the day our maintenance compound was shelled.

It was an otherwise normal day on deployment. When the shelling started, I was in my workshop. My workshop was mounted on the back of a truck and it was the size of a container you see transported by cargo ships and trains. I heard the unmistakable whistle of incoming artillery, and I heard and felt the distant impact. I grabbed my rifle and was lying under my truck within a few seconds. My truck was at the far end of the compound and everyone else was a few hundred metres away, at the other end. Our bomb shelter was also at the other end of the compound. But my truck was safely parked between two buildings, and so long as there was not a direct hit, I would be protected.

Another whistle, another impact. This time I could tell the shells were landing just outside our compound. It was quiet for a few seconds. I was not afraid, but all I had with me was my rifle. My helmet and flak jacket, extra ammunition, and all the other gear soldiers carry was still above me in my workshop. If the shelling was followed by a ground assault, I would need my gear. All I thought about was getting my gear and what to do next.

Another whistle, another impact. I braced myself for more.

I don't remember if I heard an "all clear" or if I started to move because I guessed it was safe enough. The next thing I remember is standing in the large open area at the other end

"The life of a man consists not in seeing visions and in dreaming dreams, but in active charity and in willing service."

HENRY WADSWORTH LONGFELLOW

of the compound near our bomb shelter. I was dressed in all my gear. There was no ground assault and only three shells had been fired into the field across the road. There were more people around. Some looked scared, some surprised, and a few were laughing it off the way soldiers sometimes do when no one gets hurt. I had only one thought: *I am done with the military.* I was twenty-eight, I had been a soldier for ten years, and it was time to do something else. I had a second thought: *The next ten years of my life will not be like the last ten.*

My promise to myself about the next ten years didn't feel like a goal to create something in the future; it felt like a sur-render—a letting go, or a release. I felt as though something needed to die so I could live. I didn't know what that thing was, but the acknowledgement that something needed to die, and that this would create space for something new to grow and thrive, inspired me. I felt that a new, better future was rushing toward me.

I realized that I was standing in the middle of that com-pound only because I needed a job and the military was the only job I knew. I realized that, for me, the military had just been a way to make a living. Even though I was serving my country on a mission that was important and deeply meaning-ful, and even though I would be promoted soon and my career was going great, I knew it was just a job. With blazing clarity, I understood it was a job that was still making me miserable, and it was a job that might get me killed. I wasn't afraid to die in that moment, but I didn't want to die locked into that career. I am thankful every day for everyone in uniform who serves their country, but it wasn't the job for me anymore.

All the deeply meaningful experiences were still important to me, but the meaningfulness of the job that I had dedicated myself to for ten years evaporated as I stood in the middle of that compound. I wanted out. In that moment, I decided to apply for a release from the military as soon as the deployment was completed.

When I arrived home after my deployment, I had no idea how I was going to change my working life. I was afraid of quitting only to find out I couldn't do anything else. I didn't want to have another desperate night in a hotel room like the one I'd had years before. I needed to find an employer who valued my technical knowledge and military leadership experience, but I had never even written a resumé.

Luckily, I was living in western Canada, where there were always jobs for young men willing to work hard. I got a job working on a drilling rig. On my first morning, I took off in a small airplane with the rest of the rig crew and we landed in Fort Nelson, British Columbia. An hour later I was wearing coveralls and getting dirty. It was minus twenty-five degrees and I had never worked so hard.

At that time in western Canada, working on a drilling rig was one of the highest-paying jobs you could get without much education or experience. The company didn't care that I had high-tech electronics skills or years of military leadership experience. To them I was a reliable, hard worker who didn't complain. The rest of the crew were the same. We worked hard for two weeks, made thousands of dollars, then took a week off before we did it all over again. I was becoming part of the "self-made man" story of western Canada. Boys

"It is better to be born lucky than rich."

PROVERB

were made men by working as loggers, miners, ranchers, and roughnecks, and now I was one of those men. I was part of the fabric of the land and the salt of the earth. My job had a solid, durable meaning that I could hold on to. I wanted to do that job for as long as I could—but that commitment changed on the day of the accident.

About nine months into that job, and only a week into working with a new crew on a rig positioned about a two-hour drive from my home, we had what is now called a near-miss event. "Near-miss event" always sounded too benign to me. I still call it an accident, but maybe it should be called a "nearly killed event."

I was standing in the middle of the rig floor and working on a large pipe that came up to my waist. All the heavy machinery that is normally suspended over the middle of the rig floor was winched off to the side. My supervisor wasn't paying attention and accidentally released the largest piece of machinery. Somebody yelled and I jumped to my left. A ton of iron immediately swung to the middle of the floor and crashed into the pipe I had been working on. There was an eardrum-bursting clang of metal on metal and the whole rig shook. If I hadn't jumped out of the way, I would have been chopped in half at the waist—sheared clean. My hips and legs would have dropped to the floor and my torso would have landed on the other side of the pipe.

Everybody ran to the rig floor when they heard the crash. We all looked at each other. We were amazed that I was alive and in one piece. After an accident like that, going to the bar is what rig crews did in those days, so that's what we did. I wasn't sure if my supervisor felt bad or if he was hoping I wouldn't report the accident to head office, but he bought me beer all night. Everyone seemed to take the accident in stride, as if it was the kind of thing you should expect to happen every now and then. Shaking it off and getting back to work was what tough rig hands did. I remember thinking that accidents like that can't happen every day.

The next morning, everyone started working and no one said anything about the accident. My first job that morning was to help a truck driver unload pipe. The driver pulled his truck up to our pipe racks and I began positioning the heavy lumber between the truck and the racks. Once the lumber was set, he would release the load of pipe and it would roll across the lumber and onto the racks. The most dangerous part of that job was working between the truck and the racks. If he released the chains that secured the pipe to his trailer before I finished laying the lumber, I'd be crushed. Clear communication between the driver and me was critical and I thought we had accomplished that, but just as I was positioning the last piece of lumber, he unchained the load. I heard the chains release and I jumped out of the way. There was another deafening clang of metal on metal as tons of pipe crashed to the ground. My muddy footprints were buried under the pile of pipe.

The driver hurried over to see if I was okay. He apologized over and over. I looked at him. I wasn't angry and I wasn't scared. I knew how lucky I was. That was strike number two in two days, and I wasn't hanging around for strike three. I turned, walked to my truck, and drove away without telling anyone I had quit.

Sometime during the two-hour drive home, I got scared. I feared I would never find another good job. Then I realized that the job that made boys into men wasn't made for me. For the second time, meaningful work evaporated. But I was living in Calgary, the headquarters of Canada's energy industry. When I was on the rigs, engineers and other specialists would occasionally fly in from Calgary for a day and do fascinating technical work. They were educated professionals who did not do the back-breaking, manual labour that soaked me in sweat. I must have developed a little confidence by this time, because I thought that if I could leave the military and get a well-paying job, maybe I could leave the drilling rigs and become one of them.

I was still wearing my dirty coveralls when I pulled into the parking lot of the Southern Alberta Institute of Technology. It was June and classes were out for the summer. I walked into the administration building and saw a bulletin board. On it was a list of programs for the coming school year that still had vacancies. I applied and was accepted into an engineering technology program. I believed I was destined for a safe corporate job that would see me through to retirement.

I had barely graduated high school, but at twenty-nine years old I got straight As in college. There, I also met my future wife, Joanna. The day after I graduated, I started my first corporate job and was given an office in a downtown office building. A week later I was managing my first high-tech automation project. I worked with smart women and men who treated each other with respect. I became an expert in my field, and my work took me to Europe, the Middle East, and

Asia. At one time, my business travel enabled me to fly completely around the world in one week, with stops for meetings in Canada, England, and Korea. It was exhausting but exciting. Joanna also had a great job and we soon bought our first home. My parents were so proud of me. Only one other person in our entire extended family had any education past high school, and no one in our family had a big corporate job that paid for business travel around the globe.

Years passed. I looked happy and successful, and I believed I had all the things that made for an exciting, fulfilling, and productive life. Although I was successful at my job, I found it stressful. Projects never proceeded smoothly, customers were never completely satisfied, and the support from my suppliers, teams, peers, and leaders wasn't always what I needed it to be. But all of these things that I wished were better were the normal challenges that my peers also had to overcome. Managing and overcoming challenges was what we were paid to do. And the better I was at it, the more I was paid.

I was good enough at my job, but the stress was becoming too much. I would lie awake at night worrying about my projects. I routinely lost one night's sleep each week, and some weeks I wouldn't sleep for two nights in a row. I was anxious and sometimes angry. I began to care less about doing my job well and more about how much money I could make and how much fun I could have spending it.

My focus shifted away from work toward a hobby that had become deeply meaningful: mountaineering. About six years into my high-flying corporate job, Joanna and I had started rock climbing. Soon we were climbing steep walls of ice in the Canadian Rocky Mountains. Later, we climbed bigger mountains that required a range of technical skills we developed as rock and ice climbers. We climbed on our own and sometimes with professional mountain guides. Where we lived, the climbing and mountain sports scene included a tight-knit group of dedicated outdoor enthusiasts. I was slowly becoming one of those people. I began to plan my life around climbing. My goal was to save as much of my big corporate paycheque as I could so I could retire early to a life of adventure and travel the world to climb.

My first big climbing trip was to Peru. There were three of us on that trip: me, Joanna, and Aaron, who was our good friend and a professional mountain guide. After arriving in the town of Huaraz, we spent a week doing acclimatization hikes before trekking to our base camp in the Ishinca Valley. After setting up base camp, we climbed a mountain called Urus. Urus was just over 5,400 metres high. As far as difficulty is concerned, it was an easy walk at high altitude with stunning views and great friends. We would be climbing Mount Ishinca—just a little higher, at 5,500 metres—the next day. I expected another easy, wonderful day.

We left base camp early the next morning while it was still dark so we could walk on the frozen crust of snow before it melted and softened and made travel difficult. When the sun came up, we were already high on the mountain. The higher we climbed, the worse I felt. I remember feeling nauseous and constantly trying to catch my breath. I had felt great the day before while climbing Urus, but on Ishinca something was wrong.

I don't remember everything about the climb, and Joanna still fills in gaps whenever we talk about it. But I remember feeling sick and tired. Joanna tells me I was grumpy and that I said some nasty things. Becoming belligerent and acting like a giant jerk is one of the first signs of severe hypoxia: insufficient oxygen to the brain. The minor effects of high altitude, such as nausea and headaches, are symptoms of something called acute mountain sickness (AMS). I had never exhibited any of these symptoms until I started climbing Ishinca.

Before Ishinca, I thought I had acclimatized well. Joanna often tells me that she thought I had acclimatized better than both her and Aaron. Climbers often take Diamox (acetazolamide) to mask the adverse effects of AMS while they acclimatize. Both Joanna and Aaron had been taking Diamox, but I didn't because I had felt so good. But as I became angrier, nauseous, and weak, I was moving beyond the symptoms of simple AMS and heading toward high-altitude cerebral edema (HACE). Although HACE is not fully understood, scientists agree that the symptoms associated with it, which include disorientation, hallucinations, and difficulty breathing, are caused by swelling of the brain. Without quick and adequate treatment, HACE is often fatal.

We reached the steep snow slope just below the summit and set an anchor to secure ourselves to the mountain. Aaron was the first to climb to the summit. Once he made it to the top, he would set another anchor and bring in the rope while Joanna, then I, followed. As Aaron climbed and as I fed him more rope, Joanna remembers that I looked strange. She says my skin was pale and I was sweating a lot. I remember feeling

"It isn't
the mountains
ahead to climb
that wear you out;
it's the pebble
in your shoe."

MUHAMMAD ALI

light-headed, as if I was taking microsleeps. My brain kept going completely blank for fractions of a second and I knew something was wrong. I tried to focus.

After Joanna followed Aaron to the summit, there were two tugs on the rope, signalling me to start climbing. It was less than 60 metres to the summit, but I remember thinking that I wasn't going to make it. The sun had turned the supportive crust of snow into mounds of slush. Every time I kicked my climbing boot into the slope and transferred my weight to that leg, I would sink almost to my waist. It was a blank-headed, sweaty slog. I eventually reached up and swung my ice axe into the firm snow of the summit and stood with Joanna and Aaron. Aaron said, "We made it." In my HACE-induced, belligerent fog, I said, "It's about fucking time." Their smiles dissolved. I was oblivious to what was happening, and it was about to get worse.

I don't remember much about being on the summit. I know that we weren't there very long. After a short rappel off the shaded side, we were walking on the gently sloping glacier that would get us off the mountain and back to base camp. As I walked, I became more and more disoriented. I was having difficulty breathing. I took a few more steps and my mind went blank. I stopped walking. Then I stopped breathing. I looked to my left and saw two yellow figures drift up and away from me. I knew that, somehow, those figures were me and I was leaving my body. I began gulping and biting at the air and I thought, *If I don't start breathing, I'm going to die.* Then I made a sound. It was a quiet grunt at first, but it got louder. I began yelling. I wasn't saying words at first, but the yelling made me breathe. Soon, I was yelling at Joanna and Aaron. I was trying to tell them that I couldn't breathe.

They understood I was having problems breathing, and Joanna asked Aaron if we had brought the dex (dexamethasone). Dex is a poor choice for the prevention of simple AMS—Diamox is far safer—but dex is used to reduce brain swelling and can be a lifesaver when dealing with HACE. Whereas Diamox is a pill, dex needs to be injected. It's common for climbers on big mountains like Everest to each carry a syringe or two of dex. We had brought dex with us to Peru, but since everyone, including me, appeared to have acclimatized so well prior to climbing Ishinca, we had left it at base camp.

At some point I became coherent enough to ask to be put at the front. It was an easy walk on a crevasse-free glacier, and Joanna and Aaron thought being at the front would help me focus and allow them to keep an eye on me. I walked and yelled as Joanna and Aaron followed on the rope behind me. With each descending step I could breathe a little better. The old saying that you can taste the oxygen is true. As soon as we stepped off the glacier and onto the trail that would take us back to base camp, I broke down. I sat on a rock and started crying. I hadn't cried like that since the night before I rejoined the military. I felt as though I was releasing something. I'm still not sure what it was, but I had to keep crying until it was out.

Aaron ran back to camp to make sure there was lots of drinking water and tea ready for when Joanna and I arrived. I was disoriented for much of the hike back to base camp, but Joanna took care of me. She steadied me so I wouldn't stumble off the trail and she made sure I kept moving even though all I

"Work is not man's punishment. It is his reward and his strength and his pleasure."

GEORGE SAND

wanted to do was sit and rest. At one point I turned to her and said, "I feel better." By the time I got to base camp, I felt good. After eating, I felt really good. After a couple beers, I felt great.

We all talked about what had happened. We understood it was a relatively minor case of HACE. I started taking Diamox. Aaron and I agreed to climb the last mountain planned for our trip, Tocllaraju, the next day, but we never did. A climbing party from France had fallen through a snow bridge near the summit of Tocllaraju on the day we were climbing Ishinca. The route to Tocllaraju's summit would now be too difficult for me, so we decided to go back to town.

Soon after that event on Ishinca, the stock market crashed. I didn't lose much money, but I lost hope. I would have to work for longer than I wanted. Reaching early retirement had been a kind of finish line. My goal had been to cross it as quickly as possible so I could start living more deeply immersed in meaning. Meaning was going to come from a life of travelling the world to climb mountains.

But as I became increasingly dissatisfied with my job, I soon realized that climbing had been a way for me to avoid thinking about work. My previous two jobs had nearly killed me; now, with mountain climbing as a distracting hobby, I could have died escaping from work. Work had meant an early retirement to a life of climbing, but now, for a third time, the meaning of my work evaporated. Something needed to change. I said the same thing to myself that I'd said after the shelling: *The next ten years of my life will not be like the last ten.*

In the military and on the drilling rig, I had been shown how unpredictable life was and how uncertain our time of death can be, and I was hiding from all of it. Each time I was almost killed at work, I just got another job. I thought each new job was safer and more meaningful than the last one. Each time, after I saw how I could be easily and instantly turned into a corpse, I still avoided taking a thoughtful, critical, and sobering look at how I was living my life, and instead I simply filled my world with different work. After the incident in Peru, I realized that I had only been swapping out the contents of my world instead of changing how I was being in my world.

Working for Life

When climbing lost meaning, work lost meaning. I was close to falling into a deep depression, but instead of becoming depressed, I became curious. I read book after book about work, life, and death. About a year after that day on Ishinca, I asked myself, what if I could find work that I would joyfully do until I died? What if I loved it so much that I wouldn't want to stop? What if I could happily erase the finish line?

I began taking psychology courses by distance learning. One was about career development theories. Halfway through that course, I knew I'd found my new working life and mission: to create a world where everyone has the knowledge, skills, and desire to create a deeply meaningful working life and build thriving organizations. Those courses and my new mission propelled me into my next career: helping companies create thriving workplaces, and helping individuals build their own deeply meaningful working life. I started the coaching and consulting practice that I run today. And in this new work, about work, I have found my own deeply meaningful working life.

Telling your own story

No matter where you are and what you have done in your working life, you have a story to tell. By remembering and reflecting on your story, you will begin to notice how much you already know about the meaning of work and how many challenges you have already overcome. You'll see who has influenced your journey so far, and how. You'll also become aware of how you want to change your working life, or change how you feel about the meaningful work you are already doing.

In case you are not sure how to begin, here are a few prompts:

- How did your parents or other adults talk about work when you were a child?
- What did you want to be when you "grew up"? Did it happen? Why or why not?
- If you've quit a job, why?
- If you have had one job for a long time, what keeps you there?

"Life shrinks or expands in proportion to one's courage."

ANAÏS NIN

While I continued with my education and developed my coaching practice, I stayed at my corporate job, gradually reducing my hours to part-time and then zero. But for those ten transitional years, my job was not as stressful as it had been for the previous fifteen. I found myself being more successful at my job, and happier. How could that be? How was I getting more done, getting it done better, and creating healthy teams? Why was I thriving and creating thriving teams in the same organizations where I had been miserable?

I was more successful and happier because I had learned how to thrive in three relationships we have with the work we do and the greater world of work. Understanding these relationships enables us to create our own deeply meaningful working life that is uniquely our own. The relationships are:

1 **Authentic:** discovering the work we still want to do after we understand how others have shaped our values and beliefs about work.

2 **Responsible:** contributing to well-being through our authentic work is our greatest motivation to succeed.

3 **Intentional:** achieving our vision of a deeply meaningful working life by acting with intention, every day.

WE ALL CRAVE meaningful work. Whether you are facing important first-career decisions or have been working for decades, you know that doing meaningful work contributes to your well-being. Maybe you already have work that you find meaningful, but there's something holding you back from feeling really good about the work you do. Appreciating the meaning of work in your life, and then creating your own deeply meaningful working life, is what this book is about.

Chapter 2 shows that understanding how early humans first made something meaningful—culture—helps us understand how we created the rich and diverse world of meaningful work we have today. But, because the meaningfulness of work is something that we learn from the powerful influences we encounter throughout our lives, Chapter 3 shows how you can challenge these influences and discover the work that is uniquely meaningful to you: your authentic work. Chapter 4 shows how doing your authentic work responsibly will provide your greatest motivation to succeed at that work. Chapter 5 shows how to plan and complete intentional actions that will create your deeply meaningful working life. Once you begin to change your own working life, you may wish to extend this authentic-responsible-intentional approach to your team; a resource in the appendix will help your team do their best work too.

This book is an invitation to challenge your beliefs about work and to courageously change your working life. I will guide and support you through that change in the same way that I have guided and supported my clients. If you're afraid that a change to your working life might negatively impact the lives of people you care about, don't be. The chapter on your responsible relationship with your work shows how you can contribute to the well-being of others regardless of the work you do. All the good that you will do for yourself and others starts with the courage to change. The world needs the change you'll make, but what change is right for you?

The change that is right for you, the change that is uniquely your own, is the authentic change. But making that authentic change is one of the most difficult things you will ever do. Why? Because any journey toward your authentic work begins by uncovering all the barriers to meaningfulness created by you and the world around you. As you'll see in the first chapter, we are taught the meaning of everything around us, including the meaning of our work. Understanding how humans first made something meaningful will help you understand how you can create a more meaningful working life.

2

The Meaning
of Work

T'S OFTEN SAID that the world of work exists in two ways: there is work as a means to an end, and there is work as an end in itself. First, let's look at work as a means to an end.

Thinking about work as a means to an end helps us understand the purpose of work and the motivation to work, and it's something that many people can easily talk about. For example, we can plant seeds and weed a garden (the means) in order to grow carrots for the dinner table (the end). We can operate a carrot farm to create income and wealth (the means) so we can transact in the greater economy, pay for our children's education, and pay for other goods and services (the ends).

In his book *The Psychology of Working*, David Blustein described three primary motivations for work.

His first motivation is *working as a means of survival and power*. He explains that, for most people, working provides the means to obtain the goods and services they need to survive. We work to obtain everything from basic survival needs, such as food and shelter, to more complex needs, such as education and medical care. One outcome of working to survive is the gradual accumulation of economic, social, and psychological power. Having more power in any society means that we are able to access and leverage additional resources not available to those less successful at surviving in that society.

His second motivation is *working as a means of social connection*. Work has long been a way of connecting with family, our community, and our broader social context. Through work, we are connected to our economies, political systems, cultures, and many of the people in our lives. Meaningful relationships with our co-workers make us feel safe and secure in the face of workplace and personal stress. In our current world of work, for example, there is a lot of discussion about how some of the healthiest organizations recognize that many people want a best friend at work. These social connections also help us cope with workplace stressors such as organizational restructuring or finding a new job.

Blustein's first two motivations sound a lot like working as a means to an end. Before I discuss his third motivation for work, let's think about work being an end in itself rather than only a way to survive, accumulate power, or foster social connections.

If someone's work provides for all of their needs, then how could they be dissatisfied with their work? And why do some people continue to work long after they have met all their own

"Labour for labour's sake is against nature."

JOHN LOCKE

needs, and after they've provided for others? Remember that work as a means to an end tells us the purpose of work or the motivation to work (planting carrots to feed ourselves). But purpose is different from meaning. When we say work can be an end in itself, we are saying that work has some meaning aside from the money, goods, or services we get in exchange for our work.

Blustein bases his third motivation for work on the framework provided by self-determination theory (SDT). SDT is a broad theory of human behaviour proposing that humans have inherent tendencies toward growth, and that our behaviour is aimed at satisfying our needs for competence, relatedness, and autonomy. Blustein doesn't specifically describe work as an end in itself, but his discussion takes us well beyond a simpler means-to-an-end idea of work.

Blustein makes a good argument for his third motivation for work—*working as a means of self-determination*—but other theories of human behaviour also explain why we work. One theory, developed in the 1980s, is based on the work of the Pulitzer Prize–winning cultural anthropologist Ernest Becker. It's called terror management theory. Although "terror management theory" sounds like a strange name for a theory that describes meaningful work, I'll show you how it does a great job of explaining why we ever created a world of work in the first place. And terror management theory, or TMT, can tell us why work has such power and meaning in our lives.

How Our World of Work Happened

To understand the influence and meaning that work can have in our lives, it's helpful to first understand how we created meaning and, eventually, cultures of meaning, including meaningful work.

You've likely heard it said that humans are unique because we are social animals. Sociality is the degree to which animals form social groups and co-operate within those groups. But scholars are trying to understand how human sociality is different from the social behaviour of other animals. For example, can we compare the social behaviour of a wolf pack to our own? And if other animals exhibit sociality, is there something else that makes humans unique? In the context of this debate, terror management theorists say that humans are unique not because we are social animals but because we are cultural animals.

You've also likely heard it said that humans are meaning-makers. What is more accurate is that we are meaning-*takers*, and all meaning is made available to us through our culture. From birth, we are taught, whether lovingly or hostilely, intelligently, or ignorantly, the culture that transmits the meaning of our world. For example, before we are married, we learn that marriage can mean love, stability, comfort, commitment, servitude, or abuse. Before we have children, we learn that having children can mean joy, care, responsibility, legacy, conformity, or poverty. And before we have a job, we learn that success at work can mean competence, security, wealth, power, stress, or greed. Green means go, red means stop. Our cultures teach meaning.

In our childhood, our parents, teachers, and other people in powerful positions tell us the meaning of what we see, hear, and say. As we grow into adulthood, we may devalue or ignore what our parents or teachers told us, but other people, and influential social forces like the media, continue to tell us the meaning of our world. Even when we have our own experiences with marriage, raising children, or working, we still choose the meaning of those experiences from our previously learned list of meanings provided by our culture. As you'll see later in this chapter, our culture, that master transmitter of meaning, makes it difficult for us to experience anything in a fresh way. Instead, we experience the meaning that our culture has already taught us.

Culture is the norms of human social behaviour within a society—it's what we and others think we should or shouldn't do. Culture also includes the technology, art, architecture, and systems that come about because of that behaviour. Our culture provides a perspective called a cultural world view. That cultural world view is like eyeglasses that we never take off. All that we understand about our world is filtered through and transformed by those glasses.

The easiest way to understand culture is to think like a cartographer—a map-maker. Imagine there were maps of Earth before humans existed. Those maps would not show international borders, buildings, roads, or names of lakes. All these maps would show is the untouched land and water. All the stuff that is omitted from those imaginary maps—and the impacts of that stuff, including cities and homes, factories and jobs, churches and religious beliefs, schools and exams—all of that is culture.

But why bother with culture in the first place? Why ever build anything? Why would we do anything other than what we were doing before we invented culture? We can explain why certain parts of our culture have come about—why a road was built or a city was settled, why a portrait was painted or a poem written—but why did we invent culture in the first place?

Scholars often explain culture as something that happened over a relatively short period within the timeline of human development—all of a sudden, there it was. Psychologist Julian Jaynes said, "Culture and history and religion and science is different from anything else we know of in the universe... It is as if all life evolved to a certain point, and then in ourselves turned at a right angle and simply exploded in a different direction." Although Jaynes does a great job of telling us *what* happened, he doesn't tell us *why* it happened. As with all big *why* questions, there are theories that complement and contradict each other, and it's here that terror management theory helps.

Life before Culture

Most people would say that the thought of being torn apart and eaten by hungry lions is terrifying. But we weren't always afraid of being the king of beasts' next meal. At one time in human development, we weren't even aware that we could die. Our eventual awareness and fear of death was a necessary adaptation, and with it came the creation of culture, the thing that makes us so different from other animals. Although most of us don't have to worry about being eaten by lions, many of our decisions about work are still driven by some terrifying, ancient lessons.

Let's imagine a couple of the earliest humans, and let's name them Grunt and Lurch. Grunt and Lurch are more ape than human, and spend most of their days collecting food and protecting themselves from predators. They don't have any language yet and they don't use tools. They have no system of trade, no art, or any other culture that we could point to on a map and say, "Humans are here."

It's a sunny day, between 5 and 10 million years ago, on the grasslands of what is now Africa. Grunt and Lurch have just climbed a tree to eat some fruit. They're making contented sounds as they pluck the ripe fruit and sink their sharp teeth into it. Grunt sees a piece of plump, juicy fruit that's a little out of his reach, so he swings over to a smaller branch and reaches way out to grab it. Suddenly, the branch breaks and Grunt falls, crashing through the lower branches, and hits the ground with a dull thud. Immediately, three hungry lions that were resting in the shade of a nearby rock spring into action. In less than a minute, Grunt is torn apart and devoured. Lurch watches the lions rip Grunt apart and eat him. All that remains of Grunt is a few drops of his blood in the scuffed-up dirt.

What did Lurch do next? Based on our observations of other animals, it's likely that Lurch made a lot of noise. He may have climbed higher into the tree. But, shortly after the lions left, Lurch probably went back to eating the delicious fruit as if nothing happened. Most animals, with some notable exceptions such as elephants and wolves, appear to just carry on with their lives after witnessing death.

Beginning about 3 million years ago, humans began walking upright, living in larger groups, and reflecting on their existence. Grunt and Lurch's modern cousins developed complex brains and realized that the death that happened to someone else would one day, whether by lions or some other means, happen to them. But were they paralyzed by a fear of death, and the terror they felt every time they thought about being nothing more than lion food?

Let's call Grunt and Lurch's more modern cousins Gary and Larry. If Larry witnessed Gary's death and was then paralyzed by the fear of death, maybe, as a small group of his tribe was going hunting, he would poke his head out of his cave and yell, "Why do you bother hunting for food? Don't you know that you're nothing more than lion food? All your hunting and gathering isn't going to save you from the lions." Then the hunters might say, "We hunt not just for ourselves, but for the entire tribe. The food we bring back will feed our mates and children." But Larry shouts from the cave, "You're wasting your time, they're all going to die too. Nothing matters. We're all doomed!"

Being paralyzed by a fear of death does not mean hiding from or denying death; it means being unable to find meaning in anything in the face of death. Luckily, our ancestors didn't become paralyzed. They didn't poke their terrified faces out of their caves and tell everyone that they're doomed. Why? Because around the same time that they were beginning to reflect on the nature of their uncertain existence and their inevitable death, they created culture.

Here Comes Culture

Humans began to create culture about 3 million years ago by way of something called behavioural modernity. Behavioural modernity is the development of abstract thought, co-operation in groups beyond our kin, the development of social norms, art, and the mastery of various technologies and phenomena, such as blades and fire. It's the beginning of culture. But what did the realization of their eventual death, and the accompanying terror whenever they thought about it, have to do with the creation of culture? And what does the creation of culture have to do with meaningful work? Gary and Larry can show us.

About 3 million years ago, as Gary reaches out from that smaller branch for the tantalizing fruit that's oozing with flavour, the branch breaks and he crashes to the ground. Larry watches in horror as Gary is ripped apart and eaten by the hungry lions. Larry is terrified that the lions will see, smell, or hear him and include him in their meal. Thankfully, Gary is enough for the lions and they wander back to the shade. But Larry clings to a branch near the top of the tree for hours. He waits for the lions to leave so he can run back to the protection of his cave. Larry is thinking how that could have been him, torn apart and eaten by the lions. Just one little slip and he could be lion food too. And then what? At this point in human development, there is no belief in an afterlife, and Larry hasn't developed the belief that his children will keep him "alive" in their memories long after he's dead.

When the lions stretch and then trot off to the watering hole a mile away, it's Larry's chance to escape. He shimmies down the tree and sprints back to his cave. Soon he's sitting at the back of the cave and huddling around the fire with his other cave mates. He's still shaken by the horror he has witnessed. He's afraid that what happened to Gary will happen to him and his children. Then something new happens. Larry presses his hand into the mud on the floor of the cave, stands up, and presses his muddy hand to the cave wall. There it is, a handprint, something real. Something that no lion can take away from him. If he's killed by lions, he'll be remembered when anyone sees the handprint. The handprint will exist even when Larry does not. Eventually, all Larry's cave mates dip their hands in the mud and press them to the wall.

When Larry thinks of his own death, he feels better knowing that he'll be remembered every time someone sees his handprint. The meaning of the handprint gives Larry courage to leave the cave and carry on with his perilous existence. As time passes, his tribe develops the belief that if a member dies an honourable death, they go to a world filled with fruit, game, and fresh water. Larry's life, and life itself, is now rich with meaning, as is death.

Earlier I said that our culture makes it difficult to experience anything directly. Instead, we experience the meaning provided by culture. Before Larry pressed his muddy hand to the wall, he already had a direct experience of Gary's death in the instant he saw the lions tear Gary apart. Perhaps, at that instant, Larry directly experienced Gary's death as a shaking in his body, crying, absence of appetite, tension in his neck, as time passing very slowly, and as absolute, overwhelming terror. But that terror would paralyze Larry if he was not able to make his own life, and Gary's horrible death, meaningful. The new handprint culture and beliefs about an afterlife provided a cultural world view that served as a buffer between Gary's death and Larry's direct experience of it. Without that new cultural world view, the terror Larry would experience if he contemplated being no more than lion food might paralyze him. Why bother doing anything if, at any moment, Larry and everyone he knows, including his children, could all be torn apart by lions, killed by buffalo, or have massive heart attacks, and then decay into non-existence? If that's what life means, then why bother living at all?

We need our lives to mean something if we're going to bother going on with this horrible thing called death hanging over our heads. Larry couldn't carry on with his life after seeing Gary eaten by the lions unless he could give meaning to the carrying on. Larry needed to create culture to supply life with meaning. That's the power of culture.

Larry's handprint can be called art, religion, medicine, or a job for the hand-printer, but at its core it is culture. Decades of research into terror management theory has concluded that "humans 'solved' the problems associated with the realization of their mortality by the creation of uniquely human cultural affectations, including art, language, religion, agriculture, and economics." We've created a society with a rich and diverse menu of culture powerful enough to satisfy every human's need for cultural world views and the meaning they provide. We live in a world full of culture that somehow, in the right combination or quantity, makes our lives meaningful.

Another world view—one of those uniquely "human cultural affectations"—is our world of work. And death gives work the power and influence it has in our lives.

The Culture of Work

Along with providing meaning to our lives, cultural world views also give us a way to be valued. Within the cultural world view provided by the medical profession, a cardiac surgeon is held in higher esteem than a general practitioner. Within law enforcement, being an FBI agent is more prestigious than being a traffic cop. A university will value a Nobel Prize-winning researcher over a professor of first-year physics. And within the performing arts, an Oscar-winning actor is valued more than a competent player in a local theatre production. Although few people rise to the top, all subscribers to the world view strive for legitimacy and acceptance.

In the world of work, getting a new job after competing for it against our peers feels pretty good. Earning a promotion or raise tells us that we are valued within our organization. Being given an award for making a discovery or inventing a new product are ways to be valued within our profession. But the degree to which these ways of being valued are the source of meaning in our lives depends on how immersed we are in the cultural world view provided by our world of work. So, what happens when someone or something threatens our work?

Research into terror management theory shows that weakening or threatening our cultural world views makes us more anxious. Consider how bad we feel when someone tells us that we're not good at our job. The more anxious we feel when our job performance is being criticized, or when our job security is being threatened, the more meaning we receive from having that job or from work itself. To say this another way, the

"What I do for my work is exactly what I would do if nobody paid me."

GRETCHEN RUBIN

more meaning we need from work, the worse we'll feel when that work is threatened.

But what if someone threatens the entire legitimacy of work as a source of significant meaning in our lives? How do you feel when someone tells you that your work is less important than their work? The world view that certain jobs are less valuable and less infused with meaning than other jobs is society's way of saying, "We may not give you permission to love your job."

Since this book is about work, it would be reasonable to assume that I think work should be important for everyone. But I don't. The potential for any world view to be a strong and durable source of life's meaning will vary from person to person. So, it's not that the world of work *is* or *should be* a source of significant meaning in a human life, it's that it *can be* for some people. Many people accept that certain jobs, such as being the leader of a country, a gifted artist, or a brilliant scientist, are very meaningful jobs that can, justifiably, provide a sense of self-worth. But society often withholds permission for us to find certain work (and sometimes any work) as meaningful as, for example, parenting.

If we believe that working as a pediatric oncologist is a more meaningful job than processing applications for driver's licences, then we're making it pretty hard for someone to enjoy his job processing licence applications. If we believe that one job has greater worth than another, we are denying permission for people to find their jobs deeply meaningful unless they have certain jobs. But what if we tell the pediatric oncologist that she must always find her parenting role more meaningful than her work? It will be difficult, if not impossible, for her to be satisfied in both her occupation and her family role. If the pediatric oncologist actually believes that her parenting role must always be more meaningful than her job, then every time she finds herself enjoying her work, she might feel guilty about experiencing joy.

What would society look like if raising children and immersing oneself in work were equally legitimate sources of meaning? Would parents start neglecting their children? Would doctors stop seeing patients? Of course not. There was a time, not so long ago, when Christianity provided the Western world with its sole source of meaning for human life. Every action, every day, including how children were raised, was done for God and in a way approved by the leaders of that faith. During the Age of Reason, science began to replace the Christian church and monarchies as the source of authority and legitimacy, and no one started neglecting their children because of it.

What is likely to happen if we accept the meaningfulness of work as potentially equal to that of raising children? If our history is any indication of our future behaviour, then some people will disparage the messenger because their existing world view of being a good parent is now threatened by people who think that dedicating themselves to their working lives is equally meaningful. Can both people be right? Is there room in our society for different cultural world views to equally provide the meaning we need in life?

Sam Keen, in his foreword to Becker's book *The Denial of Death*, noted that Becker's greatest contribution to humanity was that he articulated a science of evil. Becker helped us understand that all human conflict can be characterized

"Imperfections are not inadequacies; they are reminders that we're all in this together."

BRENÉ BROWN

as a battle between immortality projects: my religion against your religion, my West against your East, my interpretation of data against yours, my campaign for justice against yours, and the meaning I find in my work against the meaning you find in yours.

Although Becker's science of evil explains conflict, it doesn't show how opinions can change over time. Later in this book, I'll discuss how most people are actually wired to be good to each other. And that's why, after we wade through any opposition to the elevation of the meaningfulness of work to being merely equal to all other cultural world views, society will finally accept immersion in our working lives as equivalent to the other already socially acceptable sources of meaning. When this happens, we will finally have society's permission to live a life healthily immersed in the meaning provided by our work.

But to create the working life that is uniquely meaningful for each of us, we first need to agree to what we already know is true: working at a job, even the most mundane job, can be a source of meaning for someone that is equivalent to the meaning someone else might find in raising children, caring for their community, or any other socially acceptable human endeavour.

Equally Meaningful Work

About once a month during the first five years of our relationship, Joanna and I would meet with our friends for a meal. At these gatherings, for some reason, a group of four or five men would form, usually standing in a circle and holding a beer, and mostly talk about work. Back then, I was stressed and bored in my corporate job and beginning to immerse myself in mountaineering. As soon as two of my friends began talking to each other about their jobs, I either said something sarcastic or walked away. I now know I behaved like that because I was judging the meaning I believed they were making of their work. I thought their jobs were less meaningful than my adventurous pursuits in the mountains. Although I didn't realize it then, I now know that the meaning I thought they were getting from work was threatening the meaning I was getting from climbing. Through my behaviour, I was saying, "When it comes to the meaning of life, only one of us can be right. So, here's how I'll show you that you're wrong."

Now I understand how one person's life can be made meaningful by climbing mountains, and how another person's life can be made equally meaningful through their work, or their dedication to family, art, or music. And all work is equally meaningful, because for every job there is someone who finds that job meaningful.

Accepting that anyone's work can be equally meaningful is like saying, "I accept that I've dedicated my life to doing work that is no better, and may have no greater worth, than any other work." That can be a scary thing to admit. When you add, "Yet I still choose to do that work," you are choosing to carry on in the face of uncertainty about the actual worth of your work. It takes courage to continue on a career path that is meaningful to you while knowing that the work is no more valuable, responsible, or virtuous than other work.

Accepting that all work can be equally meaningful is a courageous act in a culture that will always tell you that being a surgeon is more meaningful than washing dishes. It is courage that enables us to discover and pursue the work that is, somehow, uniquely meaningful to us. So how, exactly, do you find that work? That's the subject of the next chapter.

3

Authentic
Work

I TELL MY CLIENTS that their authentic work is what they were meant to do from birth. Being in an authentic relationship with work is the first step toward having a deeply meaningful working life. But how can each of us discover our authentic work?

In the last chapter, I showed how our early human ancestors first made something meaningful by creating culture. Talking about how meaning is created, like so many handprints on a cave wall, can be upsetting for some. If all meaning is just made up, does anything really matter? When I came too close to death in Peru, the meaning that mountaineering provided evaporated, and with it the meaning of the job that had been funding my hobby. Each time the meaningfulness of my work evaporated, I had other sources of meaning in my life. But I still craved work that was uniquely meaningful to me.

The path toward our authentic work starts with understanding two categories of meaning—cosmic and terrestrial—and continues by examining what causes us to care about something in the absence of these two categories of meaning.

Beyond Meaningful Work

What is the meaning of life? Asking this question presupposes that human life in general has a meaning that we are capable of understanding and pursuing. Some people believe that God, a deity, or a prophet knows the meaning of life. Maybe you don't know the meaning of life yet, but you believe that something in the universe knows the goodness, evil, or meaningfulness of all that is and happens. Belief in an all-knowing person or thing represents a belief in cosmic meaning. Cosmic meaning implies a grand design by some all-powerful entity greater than ourselves. To say that human life is meaningful because of *xyz* is to believe that human life has cosmic meaning. And to say that certain work is more meaningful than other work is to believe that some all-powerful entity has also determined the meaningfulness of work.

Questions about the cosmic meaning of life solicit unverifiable answers, in that only the universe or that all-powerful entity can tell us what that meaning is. Some people believe that without cosmic meaning all things would be equal—that there would be no *truth*—but no human actually behaves as if all things are equal. Remember, we need life to mean something. Without cosmic meaning and without an ability to determine exactly what is *truly* meaningful, we need another way to make things meaningful.

Just as cosmic meaning attempts to answer the question "What is the meaning of life?" terrestrial meaning attempts to answer the question "What is the meaning of *my* life?" And as cosmic meaning asks "What work is meaningful?" terrestrial meaning asks "What work is meaningful *to me*?" It's a fine distinction, but the implications are huge. People who don't believe in cosmic meaning still manage to create meaningful lives on the basis of terrestrial meaning.

In my own journey to understand the world of work, I accepted that there might not be any cosmic meaning to work. But I also had difficulty convincing myself that any terrestrial meaning—meaning just to me—was enough to make me care about work. The question that I kept asking myself over and over was, "If the meaning of all work keeps evaporating each time I come close to death, then how can I ever find work that will remain meaningful in the face of death?" If I was ever going to find meaningful work, I needed to understand something more powerful than cosmic and terrestrial meaning.

About a year after my mountaineering accident, I realized that being a valued member in the culture of work was a potent source of my self-worth, and I began to care about one particular job.

Caring about Work

The working life that I wanted to create, which I conceptualized only after I felt that all work was equally meaningful or meaningless, was work I'd never done before. Why did I suddenly care so much about this new work that I felt was my life's purpose? Then I read, "It is care that makes human existence meaningful and makes a person's life really matter." There was the answer, in one word: "care." To care is to be human. And care in the face of meaninglessness is authenticity.

The words "authenticity" and "authentic" are used a lot today, and like many people, I often tune out when I hear or read about living an authentic life or how we should aspire to be authentic leaders. But when I read about the connection between care and authenticity, the word "authentic" took on a new and powerful meaning.

The fact that humans care shows us why we can find something meaningful even after we understand that all meaning is just a product of culture. Care shows us why contemplating our inevitable and complete annihilation at death does not stop our search for meaning. Care connects the power of death to the power of culture and our need to create meaning in a universe that may have no meaning. Care shows us that meaning is not only *out there* in the world, but something that is unique in each of us, to be discovered or created, and accepted.

For twenty-five years, my culture had told me that my meaningful work was to be found as a member of the armed forces serving my country, then as a self-made man working

"To get to authenticity, you really keep going down to the bone, to the honesty, and the inevitability of something."

MEREDITH MONK

on the rough-and-tumble drilling rigs, and then as an educated leader entrusted with millions of dollars of my company's money. But with this new understanding I could accept that I cared about work and start doing the work I cared to do. Discovering your authentic work is your first step toward creating your own deeply meaningful working life.

My authentic work is not feeding a starving continent. It's not bringing peace to people immersed in conflict that has spanned generations. Although I appreciate all of this important work, and that many people dedicate themselves to it, I came to understand that my authentic work was helping to create a world where people have the knowledge, skills, and desire to create more meaningful working lives and build thriving organizations. Someone else might believe my career isn't worth the time and energy I consistently invest in it. But that's okay, because I found my authentic work.

I had to get shelled in a war zone, be nearly chopped in half on a drilling rig, and survive a mountaineering accident before I was able to make my working life more meaningful. Luckily, there's an easier way to go about it. Here's how: If your dissatisfaction with work is making you anxious or unhappy, then the world of work is a significant source of meaning in your life. To find meaningful work, or to make their current job more meaningful, most people follow one of two paths. If either of those two paths ends in dissatisfaction, then some follow a third path to discover their authentic work. All three paths are worthy of travel if, at the end, you have created a deeply meaningful working life.

The Double-Down

If you are dissatisfied with your current work, then the first path you might consider is trying harder to convince yourself your work is deeply meaningful to you and has some purpose. Carl Jung said, "Neurosis is suffering that has not found its meaning." Giving meaning to suffering, if the meaning is powerful enough, can make suffering heroic or even joyful. So many people readily suffer in the service of a cause they believe is greater than themselves. Finding meaning or purpose in suffering through your dissatisfying working life is what I call the *double-down*.

The term "double-down" comes from the card game blackjack. A double-down allows you to drastically increase your bet (double it) with the agreement that you only get one more card (a last chance). By taking the double-down path to creating a meaningful working life, you're saying, "I'm going to increase my emotional investment in my current working life with the hope that the new meaning I give it will reduce my dissatisfaction."

Many people make a conscious decision to persevere in a job they hate because it enables them to save for their children's education, provides an income that will pay off their mortgage, or offers valuable experience that will help them get a better job in the future. Whatever the reason—whatever the meaning—the only thing that matters is that it's a good-enough reason to endure suffering. But be wary.

Sam Keen cautioned that the heroic work we undertake with the intention of creating good in the world often has the

"It is care that makes human existence meaningful and makes a person's life really matter."

MARTIN HEIDEGGER

paradoxical effect of creating harm. He meant that, although we may have the best intentions, we can cause a lot of damage along the way. If you are committing yourself to another day, year, or decade immersed in a working life that you're currently dissatisfied with, regardless of the meaning you give it, try to imagine the potential damage to yourself and others. If one of your intentions is to set a good example for others, try to imagine what they might see. What lesson are you teaching? What you do and the result is your making. James Hollis, a Jungian scholar, said that we get what we create and not what we think we deserve. Are you creating something you might regret?

When I recommitted myself to the military, I was doing a double-down (although I didn't know it at the time). The suffering I felt after failing at my dream of becoming a musician, and the piling of more suffering on top of it by going back into a career that I had fled from, would be quenched by the meaning I would create by being the best soldier and technician I could be. If you're already working, even if only for a couple of years, you've probably done your own double-down—maybe more than once. Although the double-down didn't work for me, and hasn't worked for many of my clients, it does work for some people. But what can you do if the double-down is not an option for you?

The Move-Around

The second path toward meaningful work is to change jobs with the belief that the source of our dissatisfaction lies in our current job, not in our beliefs about work itself. We find a job in a different company, industry, or country. Sometimes we upgrade our education or retrain in order to work in a new occupation or profession. I call this the *move-around*. Sometimes it takes a few new jobs, companies, countries, or occupations before we're satisfied. But if it works, then satisfied is satisfied.

When job opportunities are plentiful, many people do the move-around. Sometimes it takes only one move, other times two, before people say that their new working life is deeply meaningful. But if someone isn't satisfied after the second or third move, then they are often too exhausted or disillusioned to make another move. Soon they see that their move-arounds aren't working, and they begin to wonder if they will ever find the job that's right for them. Looking back on my own career, I see that, somehow, deep down, I didn't believe that my own move-arounds were going to work.

Regardless of my deep dissatisfaction with my military career, I was consumed with anxiety as my release date approached. The best word to describe that feeling is "precarious": feeling dangerously likely to fall or collapse. I felt as though I were wearing a layer of skin that always seemed a tiny bit too tight. Later, I thought going to college, getting a big corporate job, and advancing in my career was the kind of working life that everyone aspired to. I had made another successful career change, but the precariousness surfaced again and continued for another ten years, until I discovered my own authentic work after my mountaineering accident in Peru.

Although my move-arounds didn't work for me, yours might work for you. Changing companies, professions, or work locations are decisions you can make after gathering enough information and then reflecting on what's important to you. Your next move might be the one that creates the deeply meaningful working life that you've always wanted. But if it doesn't, then there is still one more path you can follow.

The Get-Down

After my accident in Peru, I realized that all the move-arounds to create a meaningful working life had failed. I was left feeling empty, hopeless, and completely disillusioned by work.

If you've tried the double-down and the move-around and you're still dissatisfied with your working life, then path three it is: the *get-down*. The get-down takes more effort, so it's normal to resist this option and seek shelter in the meaning provided by a world of work not of our intentional construction. It was tempting for me to avoid the moments of confusion and fear encountered along the path toward my authentic work. A few years ago I almost abandoned my journey and nearly convinced myself to take one last shot at the corporate world. I thought of getting an MBA, rededicating myself to securing bigger leadership roles in large corporations, and doing whatever I could to break into the coveted executive ranks of my industry. I thought promotions, more money, and more influence would make my work more meaningful. It was another, classic double-down.

I started to dress in a more businesslike way. I bought new suits, shirts, ties, and shoes. I began building strategic relationships with other leaders who could help me advance in my company. I got to work a little earlier and stayed a little later.

"Choose well:
Your choice is brief
and yet endless."

ELLA WINTER

But something strange was happening. My body was rebelling against the change. It started with my feet.

Before that year, I'd worn comfortable, casual shoes to the office. Now, with my new sports jackets and suits, I wore much less comfortable dress shoes. Years earlier I had injured my right foot in a climbing gym. That injury had initiated osteoarthritis. The dress shoes made walking painful, but I was committed to looking like all the other sharply dressed business people. To manage the pain, I started wearing my casual shoes to and from the office, and only wore the dress shoes at the office. It helped a bit, but I was still in pain after work, and I was developing a limp. How had I been so easily diverted from my path toward an authentic relationship with the world of work?

The get-down is not an easy path to follow. In fact, it's such a difficult path that the only way we seem to stay on it is if it's our last resort after everything else has failed. The get-down happens when we hit rock bottom in our search for meaning, when we truly feel that all work is equally meaningful or meaningless. When in that lowest of places, we ask ourselves, "If it's all the same, why do anything at all?" Asking this question means we are ready to hear the work we actually care to do. The answer comes from ourselves, not from the once-powerful influencers in our lives who had been telling us what we should do. With all the noise from society quieted, we hear the work we care to do. We hear the work that is truly our own. It may be the occupation or profession in which we are already working, or it may be a new career or business we choose to create, but it will be our authentic choice, our authentic work.

Mandy's Story

Mandy had her dream job. She was working in banking and leading a team that was developing innovative ways to engage with customers. Her job was going well—until she got a new boss. Almost overnight, her ideas and proposals were met with resistance. Her team and its work were no longer a priority for the bank. The frustration, change, and conflict made Mandy's job so stressful that she was pushed almost to her breaking point. Fortunately, Mandy was able to take a leave of absence to focus on her health.

She began her leave with a trip to Arizona. On that trip, she disconnected from social media and email. She spent her time meditating and watching the sun rise and set. Although she soon felt better, she still missed her dream job. Then Mandy heard of a retreat that required participants to be completely silent for ten days. Women and men would be separated from each other and no one would be able to read, write, or even make eye contact with other participants. At first, Mandy wasn't sure about it, but she drove the three hours to the retreat with a repeat participant. Mandy heard all about the retreat as they drove and her mind was soon put at ease.

For the next ten days, Mandy meditated for ten hours each day and took walks around the facility. During her time at the retreat, she began to understand how she had spent her working life trying to meet the expectations of others and her own high expectations so she could prove her worth to others. By the time Mandy left the retreat, she didn't want her old job back and knew that she needed to change her working life.

When I asked Mandy to describe the place of work in her life, she said, "I've realized that I love working. Work is an important part of my identity. I love building, creating, coming up with new ideas, and helping people through my work. At work, I have all these insights for business and technology, and I'm constantly amazed by human ingenuity. People talk about TGIF, getting over the hump day, and the Monday blues—I can't relate to any of those terms. When Monday comes, I'm so excited about the possibilities. I just get so much joy out of work."

At the retreat, Mandy found a way to quiet the noise from all the powerful influences in her life that were telling her what work she should do and what she should achieve. It was noise that began in her childhood and followed her into her adult relationships with work and with important people in her life. By being quiet, Mandy was able to connect with herself and begin walking a new path toward her authentic working life. She began by upgrading her skills.

"Before I got a new supervisor at the bank, I was able to be creative, innovative, and I was able to engage with our customers," Mandy recalls. "I still wanted to do that kind of work, but I also wanted to understand technology better. One problem I had at the bank was that our developers would build what I said but not what I wanted. I needed a better understanding of technology so I could better communicate what I needed people to do."

To learn more about technology, Mandy completed an intensive program in Web development and coding. A few months after I first interviewed Mandy, I contacted her to learn where her journey to create a more meaningful working life had taken her. Mandy is now a product manager with a large pharmaceutical management consulting firm. Every day, she gets to work with innovative, creative, and entrepreneurial people who have the same passion for their work as she does. Best of all, Mandy told me, "I was able to appreciate and pull together all the things I love to do the most and create a new career. I get to learn about new products, meet incredible people who are passionate about what they do, and I get to design and manage complex, creative, and innovative solutions for our customers."

Although Mandy's new job requires her to learn a new industry and use her new technical expertise, it also requires her to apply many of the competencies she used at the bank. So how did Mandy's working life actually change? Mandy's new working life is her own, intentional creation, whereas her former working life was controlled by the bank and the expectations of other people. Mandy was able to begin her journey toward her authentic work after she silenced all those expectations.

Just before Mandy left her job at the bank, she was at the lowest point in her working life. The depth of her stress, and many other negative emotions, was almost intolerable. But now Mandy is doing work similar to what she did at the bank. So why is Mandy so happy, and what part of her working life did she really change? Did she just do a classic move-around?

At the bank, Mandy was already doing a lot of the work that she loved to do, but when her new boss didn't appreciate her, she became disillusioned. Mandy was trying to live up to other people's expectations and wasn't clear about what needed to change—was it what she did, who she did it for, or the whole idea of work itself? The change Mandy made was to shake off the expectations of others and get clear about the work she really wanted to do. Now, Mandy has her own expectations for herself, and she is crystal clear about what she likes about everything she does. Although Mandy made some big changes to the contents of her world of work, what Mandy really did was to change herself.

Maybe you are like Mandy. Maybe you are already doing the work you love, but something other than the work needs to change. Maybe you don't need to focus on changing the contents of your world of work so much as you need to change how you *are* within that world of work.

Hearing the call of your authentic work

When you ask yourself the question below, pay attention to your first answer. Remember that you never have to tell anyone what that answer is. You can keep it a secret forever.

Here's the question: *Imagine you can wave a magic wand to get any job you want, and imagine that everyone will approve of that job and you will be successful. What is that job?*

(If your answer is your current job, great. The chapters on your responsible and intentional relationships with your work will help make your current work even more meaningful.)

"Fie upon
this quiet life,
I want work."

WILLIAM SHAKESPEARE,

HENRY IV, PART 1

Next, make a list of jobs that you think are more meaningful than the job you just selected. Now ask yourself what's holding you back from believing that the job you selected is as meaningful as any other job. Did you choose that job to please someone else, or are you afraid someone will disapprove of your choice?

Your authentic work is the work you choose regardless of anyone else's approval or permission. Your commitment to contributing to well-being through your authentic work is all the permission you need.

THERE IS WORK that we each care to do even after we tell ourselves that it might be meaningless to the universe. Let yourself care about work. Let yourself care about doing a particular job. If you want to care about your current job, but you are afraid everyone else will think you're silly for caring so much about what you do, remember that what you care about is your secret. Be courageous and care.

Caring deeply about our work does not come with a licence to do harm. On the contrary, it carries with it the responsibility to contribute to the well-being of everyone who could be changed by that work. As I'll discuss in the next chapter, this responsibility to minimize harm is our greatest motivation to succeed in our authentic work.

4

Responsible
Work

HOW WE DO our work changes people. Then those people go on to change what they do and the cycle of change continues. Before we know it, the entire world is changed by how we did our work. Almost every day, we learn how powerful leaders, brilliant doctors and scientists, wealthy executives, gifted artists, and popular celebrities change the world by doing their jobs in a certain way. But if we pay attention, we can see that every day regular people, doing regular jobs, are also changing the world. The changes they bring about remind us that there's really no such thing as a regular person or a regular job. Two stories from Starbucks illustrate this point.

On April 12, 2018, at a Starbucks in Philadelphia, two African-American men asked to use the bathroom, but they were told it was for paying customers only. They then sat down at a table and waited for their business acquaintance so they could all order their coffees together. The Starbucks manager saw that the men were still not ordering, so she asked them to leave. The men explained why they were waiting, but the manager called the police. The men's business acquaintance arrived as the two men were being taken away in handcuffs. A few days later, the commissioner of the Philadelphia Police Department apologized. He said he was ashamed that he and his officers had made the situation much worse. And just over a month later, for the entire afternoon of May 29, Starbucks closed eight thousand of its company-owned stores to provide racial bias awareness training to 175,000 employees.

Almost two years earlier, in September 2016, terrorists exploded three bombs in New York and New Jersey, injuring thirty-one people. After one explosion in Manhattan, as the police were investigating and the fire department was cleaning up, a different Starbucks manager began handing out free coffees and bags of food to first responders.

Each of these incidents involving a Starbucks manager was reported around the world. Some people changed their attitude toward Starbucks as a result of the incidents. The Philadelphia incident sparked protests and boycotts. In Manhattan, the acts of kindness continued with other businesses offering free pizza and free hotel rooms for those affected by the bombings. This is what I mean when I say the world is changed by the work we do, because people are changed by how we do our work.

You and I, just like every Starbucks manager, are free to do our work in any imaginable way. This means that while doing our work, we are free to behave toward others in any imaginable way. What if Starbucks managers were fully aware of their freedom? What if they were also aware of how much the world can be changed by how they do their jobs? This awareness might be so terrifying that no one would ever take a job as a manager at Starbucks. Or, it might be so empowering that everyone would aspire to be a manager at Starbucks. Either way, it's normal to feel overwhelmed, or even terrified, by such a big responsibility.

Freedom and Fear

The freedom to behave however we want is a huge responsibility. In fact, it's the greatest responsibility we have, and it can be the most terrifying burden that comes with freedom. Our freedom is the source of many of our greatest fears. Knowing that we are free to do our authentic work however we want, and knowing that with that freedom comes tremendous responsibility, can be another barrier on our journey toward creating a deeply meaningful working life. Before we address this fear, it's worth diving deeper into how freedom can cause fear. Let's look at the common fear of heights, for example.

Imagine that you are standing in the centre of the flat roof of a tall office building. It's sixty storeys tall and big enough to play football on the roof. Since the edge of the roof is so far

"The necessity of taking responsibility for one's actions represents . . . a genuine power."

WEREWERE LIKING

away, there is no chance you could fall off the building from where you are standing. Even if you took ten steps and tripped and fell on the eleventh step, you'd still be almost a football field away from the edge of the roof.

Your friend, who is standing beside you, shows you a video. The video was produced on this roof and shot with a camera attached to a helmet worn by a BASE jumper who is famous for parachuting off high-rise buildings. As the BASE jumper walks toward the edge, you are able to see exactly what she sees. You see more of the surrounding buildings as she gets closer to the edge of the roof. You see how all the other buildings are so much shorter than yours. You begin to see the streets below. Now, the BASE jumper is standing at the very edge of the roof. The camera pans down and you see that the tips of her shoes are past the edge of the roof. She leans forward and begins to fall toward the street. The video ends.

Your friend asks you to start walking toward the edge of the roof and tells you to stop as soon as you feel anxious or uncomfortable. Some people would feel anxious immediately after watching the video, and others would already have been feeling anxious from the moment they stepped onto the roof. Most people would feel calm standing in the middle of the sixtieth floor but not on the roof. Why would just going out on the roof, even without watching the video, terrify so many people? A fear of heights is common, but why do we have this fear even when there is no risk of falling?

We fear heights when there is no risk of falling because we are free. The French philosopher Jean-Paul Sartre provided one explanation. The theory goes that, while standing in the middle of that roof, you are unconsciously aware of how you are free, at any moment, to walk to the edge and jump off. You feel that unconscious awareness in your body in the same way that you'd feel a more conscious fear, like someone pointing a gun at you.

When I guided a friend through the roof scenario, he said that as long as it was a windless day and there was no one on the roof who could push him, he would feel perfectly calm. But when I pressed him to imagine walking closer and closer to the edge, he admitted he would eventually start to feel anxious. I would feel anxious too. I would be anxious even if it was impossible for me to fall from the roof.

In the same way that we are free to jump off a building, we are free to do our authentic work any way we want. We know that we are just as free to hurt someone through our work as we are to be kind to them.

Our freedom to do our authentic work in any imaginable way makes us responsible for how our work changes the world. And that freedom and responsibility can be terrifying.

Responsibility for Relationships

Many years ago, at the end of the workday, I walked through my city's downtown to go from my office to Joanna's office. As I waited at a corner for the light to change, a person who was seated against a building started shouting at me. I assumed he was shouting at me because, in that moment, he and I were the only ones on that street corner. I immediately turned to look at him. At first I didn't understand what he was saying, but it soon became clear. "You need to give me twenty dollars," he said. "I know you got twenty bucks, and you're going to give it to me."

At no point did he stand up or make any other movement that I might interpret as aggressive. He just kept shouting that I had to give him twenty dollars. Was I in any kind of relationship with that person? If so, what responsibility did I have?

Most people would say I was not in a relationship by simply standing on the street corner, and I would not have any responsibility beyond personal beliefs I might have about helping vulnerable people. But what if I were a social worker and that person on the street corner was homeless? If I were a social worker, would I have already been in a relationship with that person by the fact of my occupation? If I were a social worker and ignored him, how might that behaviour change other people? For example, someone might have seen me ignoring him and then formed the belief that social workers don't care about homeless people outside their normal work hours. Since a social worker, like anyone else, has the freedom to do his job any way he wants, I imagine that he might feel differently than I did in that situation. A social worker would likely carry an extra burden of responsibility to act in a way that made a positive contribution to that homeless person's well-being.

Saying that we are responsible for every relationship in our working life requires that we first be aware that the relationships exist, and then accept that we are responsible for the changes we can bring about. It's normal to feel overwhelmed by the idea of being responsible for the quality of every one of those relationships. It's also hard to imagine how this responsibility can be your greatest source of joy and motivation to succeed in your authentic work.

Contribution Decisions

At first, figuring out how you can contribute to well-being is probably going to feel uncomfortable, anxiety-provoking, or downright terrifying. And just as it takes courage to care about your authentic work, it takes courage to always contribute to well-being while doing that work. But why does making a positive contribution take courage? Because doing so requires making difficult decisions. They are difficult decisions because we can make a positive contribution to the well-being of others and still do some harm.

Suppose, after reading this book, someone discovers her authentic work of owning a business that manufactures beautiful stone cookware. Then, after completing a comprehensive analysis of the labour costs and workplace regulations in her own country, she determines that she should start her factory in another, much poorer country to minimize her manufacturing costs. The owner's country happens to be going through a recession and she could provide much-needed jobs at home. But in the poorer country, she would be employing some of the world's most vulnerable people, and be able to pay them a good wage and provide safe working conditions. She could also create a charitable foundation that advocated for a living wage and better working conditions for everyone in that country. But at the same time, wouldn't she also be harming people in her own country by denying them the benefit of jobs?

Some might say that the owner should take less profit so she can employ people in her own country. They could also say that consumers would be motivated to buy the stone cookware if they knew their purchase would help employ people in their own country.

Where, then, should the owner locate her factory? Is there a *right* location?

An ethical dilemma is a decision-making problem where we must choose between two motivations for action but neither motivation is acceptable or preferable to everyone. In our factory owner's ethical dilemma, one motivation for locating the factory in her own country is to patriotically provide jobs and contribute to the well-being of families and communities—and of everyone in the country, to some degree, through taxes. Locating the factory in the poorer country will contribute to the well-being of some of the world's most vulnerable people by providing a living wage, dignity, and safety. You could also say that it doesn't matter where the factory is located because, while some people's lives will be enriched by getting a job, most will simply continue in the condition they were in the day before—jobless and poor. And some might argue that no matter which country is selected, the people in the other country will be harmed.

Now imagine that the owner had already been operating the factory in her own country but was facing bankruptcy due to high wage costs and needed to move to the poorer country

"Decision is a risk rooted in the courage of being free."

PAUL TILLICH

or fold her business. That choice seems even more difficult to make.

The Daily Practice of Responsible Work

The world is full of tough choices when we become aware of the impact of our work. As I write this book, one of the many polarizing issues in North America is the construction of oil pipelines. Within Canada and the United States, there is a persistent lobby for more pipeline construction and persistent protest against construction. Each country's government flip-flops on the issue regularly. Although I'm simplifying this complex issue, it's not a trivial matter to these countries' governments and citizens. Addressing ethical dilemmas, such as whether it is better to build a pipeline or protest a pipeline, is beyond the scope of this book. But let's consider this issue through two fictional characters who are doing opposing jobs.

Melissa Melbourne is a vice-president at Cross Country Pipelines. She has worked at Cross Country for almost twenty years. She began as a pipeline designer as soon as she finished a mechanical engineering degree. Although she was one of the best designers at Cross Country, she always felt she was destined to do something different. She moved through a variety of roles at Cross Country but couldn't find a job that felt right for her. After a few months of deep introspection, she felt the call of her authentic work: Melissa wanted to lead large corporations in the most responsible way so that they could be a source of well-being for their employees and the communities in which they operated. She also wanted to be a role model for young women who aspired to lead large organizations and make a positive difference in the world doing whatever they chose to do.

When she was thirty-five years old, Melissa completed an executive MBA program and was soon promoted into a leadership role at Cross Country. Melissa was seen as one of the most thoughtful, trustworthy, and focused leaders at Cross Country. She was also known as one of the most socially responsible leaders across her industry. Two of her many high-profile accomplishments were implementing gender equity policies that eventually influenced national legislation, and establishing a socially responsible procurement program that ensured Cross Country prioritized buying goods and services from local communities.

But now Melissa is facing the toughest challenge of her career. The former executive vice-president of development at Cross Country has decided to retire. Melissa has been selected to replace him, and her first challenge is constructing a new pipeline that will transport oil from Midwest oilfields to a refinery on the west coast.

Melissa believes that the world needs to reduce fossil fuel consumption as quickly as possible and that pipeline companies need to ensure their products can be operated safely and reliably. She also believes that the jobs and tax revenues from the pipeline will contribute to the well-being of local communities and the entire country. Since Melissa has always been committed to doing her authentic work in the most responsible way, her first priority is to build the new pipeline in a way that minimizes the probability of leaks and spills, and then ensure that Cross Country has the best spill response programs in her industry. Her next priority is to convince her CEO and the board of directors that Cross Country Pipelines must develop a strategy to accelerate its programs for reducing consumption of fossil fuels both within Cross Country and nationally.

Melissa believes that, if she is successful, the new pipeline will be the most reliable and safest in the country, it will set a new standard for responsible pipeline construction, and Cross Country will become a leader in profitable transitioning away from fossil fuels and into less harmful energy sources and infrastructure.

Now let's look at the second job. Jeff Jefferies is the director of policy and community engagement at the Pipeline Action Network. After graduating from university with two degrees, one in biology and the other in chemical engineering, Jeff began working at Cross Country Pipelines. His job was to perform environmental impact assessments and prepare document submissions to various government agencies to secure approval for pipeline construction.

Near the end of his third year at Cross Country, one of the company's pipelines burst and leaked two thousand barrels of crude oil into a nearby marsh. Hundreds of birds, fish, and reptiles were killed. Crops were damaged when the oil made its way into irrigation ditches used by local farmers.

Jeff was on the team sent by Cross Country to assess the damage and meet with local landowners. When Jeff saw dead fish floating on the oil-covered marsh, he remembered how he had spent a month during his biology degree tagging fish and studying their habitat. After some deep introspection, he felt the call of his authentic work: Jeff quit Cross Country and committed himself to doing everything he could to stop the construction of pipelines and accelerate the adoption of clean, renewable energy.

Now, twenty years later, after gaining experience in some of the world's largest environmental advocacy organizations, Jeff's most important project is to stop the construction of Cross Country's new pipeline. He believes that Cross Country and the government have overstated the economic necessity and benefits of the project. He also believes that introducing more pipeline capacity will only accelerate the extraction of fossil fuels that will be sold to countries that have the highest per capita greenhouse gas emissions. Jeff believes that his country could be a leader in clean, renewable energy if the government would give it a higher priority. But Jeff also knows that many people's livelihoods, including those of his former colleagues at Cross Country Pipelines, depend on the project proceeding. He knows that many of those same people believe that focusing investment toward clean, renewable energy is unreasonable and wasteful.

Since Jeff has always been committed to doing his authentic work in the most responsible way, he develops a campaign to engage everyone whose lives will be affected by the pipeline. This includes a strategy to change the perceptions of everyone from the Cross Country management and employees to local business owners who might be hired to work on the pipeline. Jeff is always aware of the potential for actions that might

"Good people don't owe one another anything—we are one another."

DALENE MATTHEE

cause some groups to ignore his message. To address this, Jeff ensures his strategy also seeks to continually raise the credibility of the Pipeline Action Network with every stakeholder group. Also, Jeff has made members of his team accountable for developing engagement strategies that are ethical, culturally appropriate, and respectful.

Melissa and Jeff are characters I created, and unless you have worked in either of their roles, you might find it difficult to believe that each job could be done so responsibly. But do they sound too wonderful to be real? It's easier to believe that people can behave as responsibly as Melissa and Jeff once we understand why humans are inclined toward something called *prosocial behaviour*. Prosocial behaviour is perceived as generally beneficial to a group, and it's in our inclination to be prosocial where we discover the joy of minimizing harm.

Research shows that humans are more likely to be good to one another than evil. Although one person can cause misery for millions, those millions are likely to treat each other well, even in their darkest moments. But why humans are generally good has puzzled scientists for decades. The theory that we weigh the cost of helping others against the reward for helping them explains some prosocial behaviour. Another theory shows that parents and other influential people in our lives teach us that we are rewarded when we are kind and co-operative. Evolutionary scientists can demonstrate that our prosocial ancestors were more likely to pass along their genes. Studies have concluded that reminders of our own death increase our prosocial behaviour. Lastly, other studies suggest that prosocial behaviour causes our brain to be flooded with the feel-good chemical dopamine, and this might explain how prosocial behaviour can become addictive.

Why humans are prone to be prosocial, even to people we don't know, will be studied and debated for a long time, but the fact that we are prosocial is easy to see. We hold the door for someone we don't know, and tip in a restaurant that we'll never return to. Some people pay for the coffee or meal of the person in the car behind them at the drive-thru window. Most people don't have to be forced to be kind or co-operative, they just naturally want to be that way because it feels good. In the same way that caring is human, to want to contribute to well-being is human. Depending on whether you believe it is better to build pipelines or to protest against them, you likely believe that the job can be done as responsibly as Melissa or Jeff does it.

But if you believe that being completely responsible for the well-being of anyone affected by your authentic work is a barrier to doing that work, let's consider two alternatives.

Alternative 1: Avoiding Our Authentic Work

By not pursuing our authentic work, we miss one of our greatest opportunities to contribute to the well-being of others. Remember, our work changes the world. All the culture in the world—agriculture, economics, science, technology, organizations, architecture, social movements, and art—is the result of work. People worked to create everything we experience. Your work unavoidably contributes to all that humans experience.

"**Nothing strengthens the judgment and quickens the conscience like individual responsibility.**"

ELIZABETH CADY STANTON

If you've discovered your authentic work but don't want to do it because of the overwhelming responsibility to contribute to the well-being that comes with it, then what will you do instead? Will you double-down on your current job? Will you stop listening to the call of your authentic work and just keep moving around from one dissatisfying job to the next, hoping that you'll finally find satisfaction?

Alternative 2: Prioritizing Responsibility over Authenticity

You may wonder why I didn't spend the first part of this book helping people discover the most responsible work they could do. Starting like that would be based on the premise that certain work is more responsible than other work. Just as our culture socializes us to believe that certain work is more meaningful, we are influenced in the same way to believe that certain work is more responsible. So, what if I prioritized responsibility over authenticity and said that you can only pick a job from society's *Responsible Work List*? How horrible would it feel to one day become dissatisfied with your *responsible job* and then find out that there is nothing else on that list that interests you?

That's why authenticity comes before responsibility. If all work is meaningful to someone and all work can be done responsibly by someone, then why not first figure out the work that is authentically yours to do, and then commit to doing it responsibly?

Start with What

In his bestselling book *Start with Why*, Simon Sinek writes that, as a child, he wanted to be an aeronautical engineer but instead went to law school to become a criminal prosecutor. Soon, the thought of being a lawyer just didn't feel right and he discovered a career in marketing. Now, his cause, or his WHY as he calls it, is to inspire people to do the things that inspire them.

In *Start with Why*, Sinek provides one of the most informed perspectives on how other people and organizations can be incredibly effective at getting us to do what they want and buy their products. *Start with Why* is largely about developing customer loyalty by discovering why your company exists and then communicating the WHY. Throughout the book, Sinek says, "People don't buy WHAT you do, they buy WHY you do it." One of Sinek's most powerful insights is that "we are drawn to leaders and organizations that are good at communicating what they believe. Their ability to make us feel like we belong, to make us feel special, safe and not alone is part of what gives them the ability to inspire us." Giving someone a sense of belonging and meaning in their life, giving them a WHY, is likely the most effective way to get them to do something.

The world is filled with people telling us why we should do certain things. We are socialized by all the WHYs to think that certain work is more meaningful or responsible than other work, in much the same way that the most successful companies market their products to us. All the powerful influences in our lives bombard us with what we should believe and why.

"The first duty of human beings is to assume the right relationship to society—more briefly, to find your real job and do it."

CHARLOTTE PERKINS GILMAN

We are surrounded by individuals, media, and other forces trying to convince us that doing a certain job will make us feel special or enable us to belong to a group that society values above other groups. That's their WHY for doing that job. If we end up happily doing that job, then happy is happy. But I'd rather start with my *what* than their *why*.

We are able to start with our *what* only when we are able to silence all the voices that are telling us what to do and why we should do it. Those voices have created all of our beliefs and values. When we have silenced them, in that quiet awareness of our culturally constructed selves existing in a universe of culturally constructed meaning, we can finally hear what we still care to do. We hear our authentic work. We hear our *what*. Our journey toward a joyful working life begins when we hear our *what*. At that time, we are called to do our *what* responsibly.

Don't *Do* Responsible, *Be* Responsible

The best thing about doing our work responsibly is that we don't need to change what work we do. Instead, we only need to be responsible when we do that work. Put another way, responsibility is a way of being, not an extra task we do. But what's the difference between *being* responsible and *doing* responsible?

When I advanced into leadership roles, some companies provided leadership development training. Toward the end of one training session that was focused on the leadership behaviour necessary to inspire other people, the instructor asked us for feedback on what we had learned. One of my fellow leaders in the class asked, "Can you tell me how I'm going to fit all these leadership tasks in with my regular job?" I don't remember how the instructor responded, but later a quotation from Gandhi helped me answer that question and understand how we can be responsible in all that we do. Gandhi said, "Be the change you wish to see in the world." Once I thought about my colleague's question, I realized that leadership isn't a task you do as much as it is how you behave—it's a way of being.

Leaders in organizations do many things, but it's how they behave while doing those things that causes others to follow them—how they behave makes them leaders. I believe that my colleague was in a leadership role but was not actually leading people; he was probably just telling everyone else what to do. Maybe he believed that if he stopped telling people what to do, they might stop working altogether.

I believe leaders should be constantly working themselves out of a job by developing and inspiring their teams to succeed without them. Then, those inspiring leaders move on to create the next big change. If organizations don't want those kinds of leaders, then they shouldn't waste their money on leadership development. All those organizations need is managers or supervisors who schedule, allocate, and direct resources, and then measure outcomes. These people are not *being* leaders, they are *doing* management. Management is a job we do, but being a leader can be a way to do a job called "manager." All leaders manage, but not all managers lead. Similarly, someone can *do* a job without *being* responsible. People are harmed if we avoid being responsible in the pursuit of our goals. Those who are responsible in their work contribute to the well-being of others, regardless of the type of work they do.

Making your work responsible

You've likely heard of the Hippocratic Oath that doctors take. The oath to "do no harm" is a powerful instrument that greatly influences behaviour in the medical profession. Taking a Responsibility Oath, just like a doctor's Hippocratic Oath, will guide your authentic work and motivate you to be successful.

Here are three steps to creating your own Responsibility Oath.

Step 1: Make a list of potential harms that could be caused by the outcome of your authentic work. You never have to show this list to anyone. Try to list at least three harms, but no more than seven. It's important to list harms that you're already avoiding. Then, make a list of potential contributions to well-being that come about through doing your authentic work in a responsible way. Again, try to list at least three contributions, but no more than seven.

Step 2: Arrange each list in order of importance. Put the harm you most want to avoid at the top and the rest in descending order of importance. Do the same for your contributions. Each item must get its own priority—you cannot list two items as a number one priority.

Step 3: Look at your lists and reflect on the top two contributions you most want to make and the two harms you most want to minimize. Make sure that the top two on each list are the most important to you. Once you are sure, it's time to write your Responsibility Oath.

Here's the format I recommend:

While engaged in all that is necessary to [authentic work], every day in all my actions and words, I will [how you will minimize harm 1] and [how you will minimize harm 2], so that I can responsibly [contribution to well-being 1] and [contribution to well-being 2].

Here's an example of an oath for someone who wants to be the CEO of her company:

While engaged in all that is necessary **to be a successful and inspiring CEO**, every day in all my actions and words, I will **prioritize spending time with my family** and **ensure that I support my mental and physical health**, so that I can responsibly **contribute to the well-being of my family** and **be a role model for women and men who seek to balance their professional and personal lives.**

You can edit the format to make it more meaningful to you. Once you've written your Responsibility Oath, keep it in your purse or wallet, or on your phone, so you can read it any time you need a boost of inspiration.

Real People Working Responsibly

My fictional story of Melissa and Jeff and their responsible work of building and protesting pipelines helps to show that any job can be done responsibly. But how do real people behave in real jobs? Karen's and Steven's stories (they are real people, but those are not their real names) show us how contributing to well-being can be the greatest motivation to succeed at our jobs.

Karen's Story

Karen manages pension programs for a large corporation. She has worked hard to reach the top of her profession and she believes that managing pension programs is her authentic work. She is well-known in her industry and respected by her peers. But a recent setback showed Karen that the meaningfulness in her authentic work comes from doing it responsibly.

Karen had the perfect job for her: the strategic management of a billion-dollar pension plan and all the associated programs. She was the company's expert on pension legislation and management, and she was the primary contact for several external investment firms and service providers. Karen also had a great analyst, Stephanie, reporting to her. For the first few years, Karen was able to do all the things she loved to do: provide strategic oversight for national and international pension plans, manage projects, and manage vendor relationships. While she was busy with all those things, Stephanie was doing the detailed "nuts and bolts" work that makes pension programs run smoothly. Stephanie would ensure that all employee transactions (new hires, terminations, etc.) and various compliance and regulatory reporting processes were done on time and accurately, and she would answer questions from employees about their pension programs on a daily basis. Karen was glad that Stephanie enjoyed doing all the administrative tasks that Karen no longer enjoyed doing. Karen had done that work earlier in her career, but now she enjoyed having a senior, strategic role.

About three years after Karen began that pension management job, there was an economic downturn. The company had to reduce staff, and Karen lost Stephanie to the cutbacks. Suddenly, Karen had to do all her own work as well as Stephanie's. The only options were for Karen to work sixteen hours a day or do less of what she liked to do and more of what Stephanie had been doing. After all, it was Stephanie's job that kept the lights on, but at that stage in her career Karen had no desire to do it.

The first thing that crossed Karen's mind was, *I hate this*. Karen started looking for a new job right away, but roles at large corporations for strategic pension managers were hard to get in her city. Karen knew that she would be doing a lot of Stephanie's work for a while before she found another job. Then, Karen thought about all the employees whom Stephanie had helped every day. Karen thought how it wasn't their fault that Stephanie had been let go. Pension programs can be complicated, and Karen thought how those employees needed someone to explain things to them and someone to ensure their pension was well managed. Everyone in the company was being pressured to work more, so the last thing anyone needed was for Karen to be unresponsive or disengaged. When she thought about all of this, Karen committed herself to doing her job in the most responsible way.

When Karen committed herself to being responsible, something amazing happened. The more helpful and engaged she was, the less she disliked doing all those things that Stephanie had been doing. Although she still preferred strategic management and continued to look for another job, she became more satisfied with her current job. "I think the satisfaction was an outcome of all the positive feedback I got from the people I was helping," Karen recalled. "I realized that how I did my work determined how I felt about my work. When I focused on the well-being of others, my work became a source of my own well-being."

Karen's story is similar to the double-down approach to making work meaningful. Until Karen was able to find another job, she found meaning in suffering through Stephanie's tasks by focusing on the contribution she could make to others. But her story also illustrates how responsibility to minimize harm is our greatest motivation to succeed at our work. And, lastly, Karen's story is more proof that doing good feels good.

Steven's Story

Steven is a vice-president at a multinational corporation. Recent market pressures meant that the company had to reduce staff. In the first round of layoffs, Steven had to cut his staff by 25 percent. I asked Steven about the responsibility he felt and how that influenced his behaviour during the staff reductions.

"Nothing can prepare you for something like that," Steven said. In the time leading up to the day when he would have to tell a quarter of his staff that they no longer had a job, Steven was beside himself. But he also felt responsible for ensuring that the task was done as compassionately and respectfully as possible. That's when he realized the company needed the right person delivering the bad news to each employee. Steven knew his staff best, he cared for them, so he knew he was the right person for that role. "Knowing that I would be compassionate and respectful toward each person didn't make me look forward to telling them," Steven said, "but it motivated me to do the best job I could."

Steven also thought about the responsibility he felt toward the staff who would be keeping their jobs. If the company was going to survive, it needed to cut staff. Not making those staff reductions could have meant deeper cuts or even more drastic changes in the future. Steven believes that everyone in the company should be able to count on their leaders to make the best decisions and then execute those decisions in the most responsible way. Being that kind of leader is meaningful to Steven.

THE NUMBER OF relationships and the scale of possible harms and contributions that we encounter in our work can be daunting. Fear of taking responsibility for our authentic work mostly comes from a fear of not being able to minimize harm and contribute to the well-being of every person we impact. So, just as it takes courage to care about your authentic work, it takes courage to do that work responsibly. That courage is much easier to muster when we are in an intentional relationship with the work that we do. We'll explore our intentional relationship with work in the next chapter.

5

Intentional
Work

HEN MY CLIENTS discover their authentic work, many also understand how doing that work responsibly can be their greatest motivation to succeed. As their coach, I am privileged to support them every week, and sometimes every day, in doing the hard work necessary to eventually create a deeply meaningful working life.

But a handful of my clients have not been able to create that new career. Why? For a variety of reasons, they were not able to sustain their intentional relationship with their authentic work. Doing so means acting with intention every day. In this chapter, I'm going to address the most important intentional actions that made the difference between my clients creating that new working life or falling short.

Acting with Intention

To act with intention is to expect a specific outcome from your action. Intentional action is deliberate and guided. If we are not acting intentionally, then we're acting either automatically or unconsciously. Automatic actions are the daily, reactive actions that ensure our in-the-moment survival and include the routine habits of daily living. We get out of bed, stumble into the shower, and eat our breakfast without thinking too much about what we are doing. Our automatic actions while driving to work keep us safe in traffic. In contrast, when we act unconsciously, we are unaware of the consequences of our actions. Then, when the outcome is undesirable or harmful, we often say, "I didn't intend for that to happen."

To be in an intentional relationship with the world of work means taking deliberate actions in the responsible pursuit and performance of our authentic work and expecting certain outcomes. But before we can be in an intentional relationship with the world of work, we first need something that will guide our deliberate action—in other words, our intention, or what we intend to happen. Alex's story shows the importance of that guidance.

Alex's Story

After I worked with thirty-two-year-old Alex for a couple of sessions, he identified his authentic work. Although he was currently working in the accounting department of a large home electronics company, he wanted to work in the music industry as a recording engineer. Years earlier, between Alex finishing university and beginning his current job, his father had secured him a six-month internship at a music company in London. Alex's favourite part of his internship was a week he spent in the recording booth with one of the company's senior recording engineers. Alex said being in the recording booth "just felt right," and it reminded him of his university days when he worked as a DJ on weekends. Alex said the recording engineer in London frequently praised his ability to quickly learn how the equipment worked, and commented that Alex was "a natural at the controls." Although Alex next asked me to help him develop a plan to become a recording engineer, he came up with a negative counterpoint to every helpful suggestion, goal, or opportunity. I call this behaviour the *Yes, but* syndrome, and I discuss it, and other self-sabotaging behaviours, later in this chapter. Shortly after Alex began self-sabotaging, he ended our sessions.

Alex knew his authentic work, and I'm sure he would have done it responsibly, but something was holding him back from continuing to take action to change his working life. I wondered why I had been comfortable taking daily actions to change my own working life but some of my clients weren't. I realized that I had committed to the three most important elements that support any personal change: a helpful vision of the future, a helpful promise to myself, and a list of specific helpful behaviours. I call this our VPB: vision, promise, and behaviours. It's your VPB that will enable you to create and accomplish the goals and tasks that will accelerate your journey toward a deeply meaningful working life. Your VPB is developed first. Goals and tasks are developed last.

"Ultimately, human intentionality is the most powerful evolutionary force on this planet."

GEORGE B. LEONARD

Vision

A vision of our deeply meaningful working life acts as a giant magnet that pulls us through the challenges we face along our journey. Like a magnet, the closer we get, the stronger it pulls and the faster we approach it. And, just like a magnet, when we finally arrive, we become inseparable from our vision.

A vision is not a goal. Although we feel satisfied once we accomplish a goal, we soon begin creating new goals and leave the old, accomplished goals behind. A vision is not satisfying because we achieve it, it's satisfying because we get to experience it day after day. Achieving our vision means giving ourselves the opportunity to live it every day.

Vision statements created by organizations are meant to inspire and focus people within the organization (motivate employees or members) and change the behaviour of people outside the organization (attract customers or inspire a movement). These statements need to appeal to a diverse audience. But your personal vision statement only needs to appeal to you and propel you forward. Your vision will become your greatest comfort during times of stress. When I'm feeling overwhelmed by challenges in my working life, my vision helps me reframe those challenges as welcome opportunities to learn so I can move forward.

A vision statement about your meaningful working life will be most helpful when it incorporates these three elements:

- **Your vision needs to describe a *feeling* or state of being.** How do you want to feel while you are doing your authentic work? Do you want to feel satisfied, inspired, content, confident, competent, generous, peaceful, engaged, delighted, cheerful, happy, or joyous? A deeply meaningful working life will make you feel good, but "good" isn't detailed enough to motivate most people. In your vision statement, include one or two feeling words that are meaningful to you.

- **Your vision needs to describe *action*.** Your vision describes what you will be doing in the future, but it's stated in the present tense and includes verbs ending in "ing," like creating, implementing, innovating, leading, facilitating, motivating, challenging, completing, accomplishing, etc. Although we can't fully control what our work will produce—we can only try to influence the outcome of our work—we can control our own behaviour: what we do.

- **Your vision needs to be *concise*.** A concise vision provides information clearly and in as few words as possible. It's especially important that you experience the meaning of each word in your vision as immediately as possible. Choose words that capture exactly what you mean. When you do, you'll feel the power of each word, your vision will flow, and your mind won't wander as you read it. You'll need to remember your vision and be able to repeat it to yourself, so fifteen words or fewer is ideal.

Here are some examples of personal vision statements:

- **Joyfully** (feeling/state) **developing** (doing word) and **implementing** (doing word) effective social media strategies for large corporations (authentic work).

- **Confidently** and **competently leading** high-performing IT support teams.

- **Living** in **personally defined abundance** while **contributing** to a stress-free customer experience.

Promise

Like a personal vision, a promise has incredible power to guide action. And, just like a vision, a promise is not a goal or a task in that it's never finished or accomplished. Instead, we keep our promise every day. When we keep a promise, we feel competent, accomplished, and proud. While your vision describes what you will be doing and how it will make you feel, your promise describes your commitment to take the same action every day. You will make only one promise to yourself, but you must keep that promise every day.

A promise will be most helpful when it includes these three elements:

- Your promise needs to be something you can do, and want to do, every day, no matter where you are and no matter what else is happening.

"Behaviour is
the mirror in which
everyone shows
their image."

JOHANN WOLFGANG VON GOETHE

- Your promise is something you can do more than once per day.

- Your promise is something that, every time you do it, moves you toward your deeply meaningful working life.

Here are some examples of helpful promises:

- Every day, I will learn something that will help me achieve my vision.

- Every day, I will identify someone who will help me achieve my vision.

- Every day, I will challenge my values and beliefs in a way that will help me achieve my vision.

Behaviours

In recent years, physicists have advanced theories showing that our consciousness affects the physical world of matter that surrounds us. For example, they have shown that the mere act of observing a scientific experiment changes the outcome of that experiment. Although they have been able to demonstrate that consciousness can move matter at the quantum level, we are only able to understand the events and outcomes in our daily lives as a manifestation of physical action. In other words, we only experience how doing or saying something changes our world, not how just thinking about something might cause physical change.

It's important to recognize that what we do or say will cause something to happen. This recognition is both encouraging and a warning. Behaviours become habits, and habits are hard to change. So if you already have habits that will help you achieve your vision, then keep doing them. But if you need to develop new habits, then you'll first need to determine the helpful behaviour that you want to turn into a habit. It's these helpful behaviours that will cause you to keep your promise and achieve your vision.

Although you created only one vision and one promise, you'll need to commit to five to seven helpful behaviours. But, just like a vision and a promise, behaviours are never finished or accomplished. And just as you commit to keeping your promise, you will commit to acting out your behaviours. Lastly, you may have wanted to make more than one promise to yourself, but I said you should make only one important promise. Now is your chance to include those other promises in your list of behaviours.

Behaviours will be most helpful when they include these three elements:

- The behaviour should always cause an immediate, positive change in your working life, no matter how small.

- The behaviour is something that can be enacted every week, and maybe multiple times per week.

- Some of the behaviours need to be enacted with other people who will likely propel you toward your vision.

"When I dare
to be powerful,
to use my strength in
the service of my vision,
then it becomes less
and less important
whether I am afraid."

AUDRE LORDE

Here are some examples of helpful behaviours:

- I develop and nurture supportive relationships.
- I seek perspectives that challenge my world view.
- I maintain awareness of opportunities with prospective employers.
- I study [insert your authentic work here, for example: elder care, marketing, cabinetmaking, cooking, industrial design, journalism, flying, not-for-profit management…].
- I care for my physical and mental health.

Committing to Your VPB

Just as committing to doing your authentic work responsibly is your greatest motivation to succeed, committing to a clear vision, promise, and list of behaviours (VPB) is the single most effective way to begin pursuing a deeply meaningful working life. It will spring you out of bed in the morning. It will keep you focused on your tasks and goals throughout your day. And it will calm your busy, questioning mind before you go to sleep.

Now is the time to begin crafting your VPB. It will take time to get it right, and you will refine it along the way. Once you feel your VPB is good enough to move forward with, keep it with you at all times. Some of my clients have written it on a card and keep it in their purse or wallet. Some save it with their photos on their phone. Having your VPB close by will make sure you develop the right goals and tasks.

Here's an example of a VPB:

Vision: I am contributing to well-being and living in personally defined abundance while managing marketing campaigns for women entrepreneurs.

Promise: Every day I will challenge my values and beliefs in a way that accelerates me toward my vision.

Behaviours:
- I care for my physical and mental health.
- I act with integrity, respect, and compassion.
- I learn something new every day.
- I seek out, create, and maintain mutually beneficial relationships.
- I support my community.

Creating and using your VPB

It takes time to craft your VPB, and you'll probably keep rewriting it throughout your journey toward your deeply meaningful working life.

Here are some tips to help you along:

Start now: Begin writing your VPB immediately, rather than spending time thinking about it. You'll probably only get a few words down before you begin revising them, but seeing the words on the page, your phone, or a whiteboard is the quickest way to know what sounds right.

Don't include goals and tasks: Make sure you've understood the difference between your VPB, goals, and tasks. Unlike with your VPB, you'll move on to new goals and tasks after the old ones are done. But your VPB will guide you while you're completing goals and tasks.

Read your VPB first thing in the morning and last thing at night: Your VPB will motivate and calm you, because it's clear, short, and uniquely meaningful to you. When my clients read their VPB, many read it three times in a row. You can read your VPB as many times as you like—just make sure you do it at least once in the morning and once at night.

Setting Goals

Focusing on the abyss that separates your current working life from your authentic work can be overwhelming and discouraging. But setting goals and completing tasks can be calming and encouraging. Although every journey begins with a single step, a journey will only be completed if you keep stepping forward by regularly setting goals and completing tasks.

After creating your VPB, your first question might be, "How do I start?" When my clients ask that question, my answer is, "Goal Number 1: figuring out how to start." If you don't know how to begin changing your working life, your first goal is to figure that out. Then I ask, "When can you have that done by?" If their answer isn't, "By the time we meet next week," then I ask, "What part of it can you do by next week?" There's a lot you can do to gather more information about how to start changing your working life. You can research on the Internet, talk to a friend or family member, or find a book or night school course that will help you create your goals.

Your existing skills and knowledge, and your individual circumstances—such as where you live, how much time and money you have, and your existing commitments and relationships—influence the development of subsequent goals. But, regardless of your circumstances, once one goal is accomplished, another appears.

For every goal you want to accomplish after Goal Number 1, you should be able to answer yes to at least one of these questions:

- Will accomplishing this goal solve a specific problem or answer a specific question?

- Will accomplishing this goal show you what not to do in the future?

- Will accomplishing this goal show you what new goal you need to set?

"The self-confidence one builds from achieving difficult things and accomplishing goals is the most beautiful thing of all."

MADONNA

The difference between goals and tasks

Tasks are things we do to accomplish a goal. If one of your behaviours in your VPB is to attend to your physical health, then you might set a goal to lose ten pounds. To accomplish this goal, you might schedule three trips to the gym each week. Each trip to the gym is one task that will help you accomplish your goal. Once you've lost ten pounds, you'll probably want to set a new goal, like maintaining your weight. To keep the ten pounds off, you might need to schedule only two trips to the gym each week.

Your VPB will guide the goals you set to change your working life. Once you accomplish each goal, you can confidently move on to the next, knowing that your VPB will keep you on track.

Here are a few tips to help you set effective goals:

Beginning and end: You'll need to determine when to begin accomplishing a particular goal. A goal begins when you schedule the first task for that goal. A goal is completed when you have achieved the desired outcome. For example, your goal might be to get Jane Smith to hire you for one month of consulting work. To begin accomplishing that goal, your first task might be to get a friend to introduce you to Jane. Your goal would be finished when Jane pays you.

Let go of the A-R-T of goals: You've probably heard that your goals should be SMART: specific, measurable, achievable, realistic, and timely. It's helpful to set goals that are specific (knowing exactly what you want to accomplish) and measurable (being able to tell if you're making progress), but you might not know what is achievable or realistic until you try. Also, remember that the timeliness of your goal (when it should be done by) is up to you.

Be ready to abandon bad goals: Accomplishing tasks will give you more information about the goal you've set and show you if the goal will help you achieve your vision. The only thing worse than realizing you've set the wrong goal is continuing to work at it after that realization. A big part of success is noticing what's not helpful, admitting you were wrong, and setting new goals.

Completing Tasks

Accomplishing goals is how you transform the *idea* of intentionality into real, intentional *action*. But knowing what goals you need to accomplish, and being wildly motivated to accomplish them, still isn't all you need to actually get something done. You also need time to complete tasks if you're ever going to accomplish a goal. Luckily, all humans are masters at occupying their time with tasks. You're using your time right now to read this book. The task is reading this book, and the goal (hopefully) is to finish this book. A helpful outcome from reading this book would be one or more of: learning what goal to set next, solving a specific problem or answering a specific question, or learning what not to do in the future.

But if you're as busy as most of my clients, maybe a little how-to-schedule-tasks coaching is what you need right now.

"People prefer
the certainty of
misery to the misery
of uncertainty."

VIRGINIA SATIR

Scheduling tasks is not making a list of daily tasks—it's not a to-do list. Scheduling means allocating specific and adequate time during a day to complete tasks.

For example, let's say that one of your goals is to make a decision based on information provided during a phone call. If you need to make the phone call at 9 a.m., then allocate enough time to prepare for the call, enough time to complete the call, and enough time to make that decision. Your schedule might include the following: get clear on what I need from this call (8:45–9:00); make the call (9:00–9:30); review call notes and make a decision (9:30–9:45). Your thirty-minute call took sixty minutes of your time, but by scheduling these three important tasks, you actually accomplished a goal.

Here are a few more tips to help you schedule tasks:

Maintain white space: No matter how good you are at scheduling your time, unforeseen tasks are going to spring up. You can plan for this by making sure there is some extra room in your schedule, or that there are low-priority tasks you can drop from your schedule. A good rule of thumb is to leave 25 percent of your workday open or flexible.

Follow the list-prioritize-schedule method: At the end of each day, plan the next day by making a list of every task you'd like to accomplish, then prioritize the tasks on the list. Starting with the highest priority, schedule each task between existing commitments. If you run out of time before you run out of tasks, tentatively schedule the remaining tasks for the following work-day. As you get toward the end of your day, you can use any remaining white space for those extra tasks.

Immediately schedule follow-up tasks: If you need a response from an email or voice message before the end of the week, then schedule a follow-up. If you get a response before your follow-up, then cross out the follow-up when you get to it.

If you think of it, schedule it: If it's September and you want to call a prospective employer in the new year, then schedule a reminder to yourself on the first workday in January. Once it's in your schedule, you won't need to worry about forgetting that task.

Low-priority tasks never have to get done: Procrastination is one of the self-sabotaging behaviours, but choosing to ignore low-priority tasks in favour of ones that accelerate your progress is good planning. If you never get it done, no problem.

Self-Sabotage

No matter how good we are at scheduling tasks, we all struggle to accomplish our goals. The main reason all of us sometimes struggle to get stuff done is self-sabotage, or creating obstacles for ourselves. We get in our own way. I've done it, I still do it, and you will too. Although we need to overcome obstacles and influence others, our greatest resistance to changing our working lives comes from within. We sometimes self-sabotage

"Greatness is
not measured by
what a man or woman
accomplishes, but by
the opposition
they have to overcome
to reach their goals."

DOROTHY HEIGHT

when we fear failing at a goal. Self-sabotaging our journey toward a deeply meaningful working life is more easily understood if we examine the typical, step-by-step pattern:

- **Step 1:** We begin taking action to achieve our vision of a deeply meaningful working life. We might start thinking about our choices in the world of work, or tell someone how we want to change our working life.

- **Step 2:** The action causes us to experience stress due to uncertainty, ambiguity, vagueness, or being anchorless. The stress can also come from feeling overwhelmed by our freedom to choose our work and knowing how completely responsible we are for our choices.

- **Step 3:** We create obstacles and focus on one or more reasons why we should abandon our journey.

- **Step 4:** We abandon any action or plan to change our working life.

- **Step 5:** We blame others for our failure to pursue our deeply meaningful working life.

You can avoid Steps 4 and 5 by recognizing and responding to your own self-sabotaging. Here are the most common self-sabotaging behaviours to watch for:

- **Imposter syndrome:** Feeling as though you have not earned the right to pursue your authentic work is causing you to be embarrassed about telling people about your authentic work.

- **Enmeshment:** Your unhealthy over-concern for family members or intimate partners is holding you back from pursuing your authentic work.

- *Yes, but* **syndrome:** Your excessive need for people to appreciate the risks and potential negative consequences associated with pursuing your authentic work is causing you to continually offer a negative counterpoint to others' advice, praise, or interest regarding your authentic work. You usually respond to helpful suggestions with, "Yes, but..."

- **Procrastination:** Your habitual and intentional avoidance of starting or finishing a task, while understanding the negative consequences of avoidance, is causing you to dread starting or finishing a task that you know will help you create a deeply meaningful working life.

- **DIY syndrome:** Your inability or refusal to delegate tasks to, or seek assistance from, other people is causing you to feel disconnected and alone, and to believe no one else cares if you create your meaningful working life.

- **Perfectionism:** Your inability to complete tasks, or your continual redoing of tasks in an attempt to achieve a perfect outcome, is causing you to feel as though your tasks and the tasks you assign to others are never done properly.

- **Uncertainty intolerance:** Your excessive anxiety about the impossibility of adequately predicting or controlling the quality or nature of future outcomes is causing you to worry about the future so much that it is impacting your physical and/or mental health.

"The most
difficult thing is
the decision to act,
the rest is merely
tenacity."

ROBYN DAVIDSON

Responding to Self-Sabotage

Race-car driver Mario Andretti said, "If everything seems under control, you're not going fast enough." My modification of Andretti's words is, *If you don't feel the urge to self-sabotage, you're not making meaningful change in your working life.*

When you notice that you are self-sabotaging in one of the ways I've listed above, first tell yourself that self-sabotage is a perfectly normal response to experiencing meaningful change. Change is uncomfortable. Be thankful that you are beginning to self-sabotage and be super-thankful that you are now aware of it. Although there are seven common ways we self-sabotage, there are only three steps we need to take to stop it.

3 Steps to Stopping Self-Sabotage

Step 1: Read your VPB out loud. Your vision, promise, and behaviours can ground and centre you. Reading your VPB out loud gives it more power and legitimacy

Step 2: Review your goals and tasks for the week. It's normal to learn that we have established the wrong goal only after we have accomplished it, or tried and failed to accomplish it. Also, there may be goals on your list that won't help you achieve your vision. Review your goals to make sure that you really need to accomplish them. Create new goals as necessary.

Step 3: Get one thing done now! Select one task from your list and get all or part of it done in this moment. You can always do something that gets you one step closer to doing your authentic work, even if it's the smallest step you'll ever take. Doing something will make you feel good, because everything you do to accomplish your goals is guided by your vision, promise, and behaviours.

Calming the Overwhelming

My clients often say they feel overwhelmed by the idea of changing their working life—not by actions they have already taken or are about to take, but by the *idea* of change. Left unaddressed, being overwhelmed can cause us to dig deeper and deeper into our rut of self-sabotage. To help calm those normal feelings of being overwhelmed, I always offer three perspectives. And along with their VPB, it's one or more of these three perspectives that clients turn to over and over again to calm the waters of change.

Parallel Path

The instant we begin thinking about changing our working life, we may feel as if our current job, occupation, or career begins to change as well. But when we first create a plan to change, the day-to-day circumstances of our working life remain the same. Just thinking about creating a new working life does not harm your current working life. All that thinking about change does is create a safe, parallel path through your working life.

"Great things are not done by impulse, but by a series of small things brought together."

VINCENT VAN GOGH

Imagine that you are walking along a well-travelled path that wanders through a lush forest. You've been walking this path all morning and it's taken you through beautiful meadows and across hills that gave you fantastic views of the countryside. Looking ahead, you see that the path has now become two parallel paths. Both paths still appear to be headed in the same direction. If your original path was the one on the left, how will your journey be harmed if you now walk the path on the right?

Recognize that beside your existing career path you have created a new, parallel path. Accept that it's impossible to know where either path will take you. You can walk with one foot on each path, but you will eventually have to choose one direction if the paths begin to diverge. And at that time, if you choose to stay on your original path, your decision will be well-informed by what you have learned by safely walking on that parallel path.

Information before Decision

Deciding what career path to follow can be stressful if you don't have enough information. Waiting to make a decision until you have more information is not procrastination if you are actively gathering specific, attainable information. As long as you are actively seeking that information, you are moving forward in your journey.

At the Most, B, Not Z, Happens Tomorrow

Although it's true that drops of water, falling over thousands of years, will make a hole in stone, the effect of a single drop is imperceptible. I ask my clients to let their mind misbehave for a moment and imagine the most extreme, negative consequences caused by taking one action to change their working life. After they have a good laugh at the nutty things they imagine, I ask, "What's likely to happen tomorrow if you take that action today?" Of course, the outcome of that action is usually helpful, but it is neither earth-shatteringly wonderful nor terrifying. A single action is more like that one drop of water falling on stone.

Your current, dissatisfying working life is Point A on your journey to Point Z—a deeply meaningful working life. Everything you do today will, at best, get you to Point B tomorrow, not to Point Z. I know how scary Point Z can look, but Point B is your friend. Move to Point B.

ACTING INTENTIONALLY IN the responsible pursuit of your authentic work is a deeply meaningful working life. But with each intentional act comes change, and with change may come anxiety, doubt, and a tendency to self-sabotage. Anxiety, doubt, and self-sabotage are aspects of the dragon that reappears every day to block your path. Thankfully, you are fully capable of slaying that dragon each time it appears, but dragon slaying demands courage. You have that courage. Slay that dragon every day. Become an expert dragon slayer who dares the dragon to reappear, at its peril.

Conclusion

I N THIS BOOK, I have explained my approach to creating a deeply meaningful working life. Without getting shelled in the former Yugoslavia, almost being chopped in half on a drilling rig, experiencing oxygen deprivation on a mountain in Peru, rising through the corporate ranks, and spending the next twelve years learning about work through my coaching practice and academic work, I never would have developed this understanding of the world of work. But similar paths were being followed long before I "discovered" this one. And it's the lives of people like Ezzrett "Sugarfoot" Anderson that remind me of that every day.

Ezzrett "Sugarfoot" Anderson was born in Arkansas in 1920. He played on the All-American football team at Kentucky State University before he and his first wife, Virnetta, moved with their extended family to California to support the war effort. Both Ezzrett and his father worked at North American Aviation, doing whatever jobs were needed to build America's planes. But Ezzrett shifted his path—first playing pro football and then acting in films.

In 1949, he was lured out of retirement by the Calgary Stampeders to play in the Canadian Football League. In the off-season, he fronted a blues band and hosted a popular radio show. When he finally retired from the field in 1955, still a young man at thirty-five, most of his working life lay ahead of him. Sugarfoot became a heavy-duty mechanic and, after operating his own service station, maintained heavy equipment for a large local employer. Sugarfoot stayed connected to the Stampeders, and after retiring from work he rejoined the club as an account representative and respected elder statesman and mentor on the practice field and at team events.

I was fortunate to meet Barry Anderson, Sugarfoot's son. The more questions I asked Barry about his father's many jobs, the more I learned that I don't really have anything new to tell people about work. At least, I don't know anything that Sugarfoot didn't already know.

Barry told me his father didn't value one of his jobs over any other. "He would have definitely told you that all the jobs he had were worthwhile and valuable. He would have never said that being a football player was better than being a mechanic. He was equally proud of his Red Seal mechanic's licence, his Screen Actors Guild card, and his Grey Cup rings—all five of them—he earned while working for the team after he left the field."

Sugarfoot knew that it doesn't matter what job you do, as long as you are honest and do your best. And he practised what he preached. Before Barry began his own career in marketing, he wanted to be a designer and an artist, but wondered if a career in art would be worthwhile. Sugarfoot never pushed his son away from art, or toward sports or a more traditional occupation, and he reassured him that as long as he loved what he did, and worked his butt off to do it, he'd win.

Sugarfoot knew that all work could be valuable and meaningful with the right attitude. He knew that we should not do a job just because others think we should do it. He knew that we should do the kind of work we love. And, more than anything, he knew that the best job, the best life, is doing something that makes a difference in people's lives.

The End of Work

Years ago, just after my mountaineering accident in Peru, I read a popular book about living in the present moment. The book discussed the calmness we experience when we detach our mind from the past and future, and focus fully on the present, the now. When I tried the exercises recommended by the author, I felt as if I was numbing myself to daily life. When I focused my mind on the present moment, my mind emptied, just as the author said it would, but nothing else happened. It was as if I had been given a general anaesthetic for a few seconds. I didn't feel calmer; instead, I felt nothing.

"Courage is
the price that
Life exacts for
granting peace."

AMELIA EARHART

A few years later, a friend explained how it would be helpful if I could practise just *being*, instead of always *doing* something. I thought just being was impossible. No matter how much I tried, I didn't see myself as ever just being. When I think about living in the present moment, and the idea of just being and not doing, I understand these as helpful ideas, but not what humans are actually capable of. These ideas are helpful because they challenge us to slow down, calm down, so we can be more intentional. But we can't actually live in the present moment, since every present moment that we recognize immediately slips into the past as soon as we think of it. We can never grasp the present. We may be called human beings, but we're always humans doing. It's the same way with work as an end in itself.

The idea of work being an end in itself is helpful because it challenges us to think differently about the value of the work we do, and it challenges us to be conscious of our choices in the world of work. But if we actually try to imagine work as an end in itself, we soon arrive at the inconceivable. If someone's work were truly an end in itself, she would not want to benefit from the associated salary. She might donate her paycheque, saying that her work is a way for her to help others—but that's still work as a means to an end. She might say that she only works to make social connections—again, a means to an end. But most importantly, she couldn't say that just doing the work makes her feel satisfied. If the work provides satisfaction, then that's another way of saying that the work is a satisfying means to her end.

When it comes to work as a means to an end, there are no rules about what the goal of work should be. Although we don't normally say that we are working as a means to achieve survival and power, many people say they will stop working once they pay off their mortgage and have a certain amount of money in their savings account. Or they might stop working once they achieve a certain level of influence in an organization or community.

Most people don't specifically say they work as a means for social connection, but people sometimes quit their job when their favourite co-workers leave. Many people work until there is a significant change to their family. But just as we are conditioned to choose certain work, we are conditioned to choose a certain end to work. The end of work that we are most conditioned to desire is retirement.

The award-winning television commercials by London Life, a Canadian insurance company, introduced a generation to the idea of retiring at age fifty-five. One Freedom 55 commercial showed a man running to catch his bus to work, then in the next scene he has been magically transported into the future, where he is jogging along a tropical beach, all thanks to wise financial planning. But when people took a hard look at their personal economic reality, not specifically at London Life's financial products or the company's performance, they soon started to joke about how old they might be before they could afford to retire. Freedom 85 became the dark joke people would make when talking about their retirement savings.

Most people say they would retire, meaning they would stop working altogether, if they had enough money to provide for all their needs and wants until death. But it's also true that there are people who say they never want to retire and hope to keep working at their job, a job they love, until they die, or at least until they are no longer physically or mentally capable of working. Of course, there are infinite variations of retirement between and beyond these two examples. And it's these infinite variations which remind us that, just as we must each discover our own deeply meaningful working life, we must discover what end to work is meaningful for each of us.

CREATING OUR OWN deeply meaningful working life begins with the courage to cast off the judgments and expectations of others. Then, when we accept that no work is more meaningful than any other work, we still need the courage to care about our authentic work. After we courageously accept responsibility for contributing to the well-being of everyone who is changed by our work, we must commit to courageously acting with intention in the responsible pursuit of our authentic work. It takes courage to tell others about our own struggles through the world of work, and then to choose the end of work that is uniquely right for each of us. That's a lot of courage to change, but the world needs the changes you'll make. Be courageous and change your working life.

Acknowledgements

S HORTLY AFTER MY mountaineering accident, I began taking undergraduate psychology courses by distance learning. I wanted to understand myself and others, but the courses seemed only to contribute to my confusion. One course presented a range of career counselling theories, but none spoke directly to how I already experienced my twenty-year career. In my final paper, I challenged the academic status quo by proposing a new theory for career satisfaction—a risky move for an undergraduate student. Shortly after the submission deadline, my instructor scheduled a meeting with me. I didn't know what to expect, but I was relieved when he said, "You have done great work. You could do a master's degree on this." That instructor was George Joyes, and he gave me the confidence I needed to begin helping others create meaningful working lives. Thanks, George—my commitment to creating a better world of work began when you gave me that encouragement.

Although there are many paths toward publication, I am privileged to work with Page Two. The Page Two team took time to understand my goals, provide clear recommendations, and deliver brilliant editing, design, and marketing solutions. A special thanks goes to my Page Two editor, Amanda Lewis, for her competence, creativity, and kindness.

Of course, this book would not be possible without the support and contributions of many people. Thank you, Barry Anderson, for sharing your father's inspiring story. Thank you, Amy Lister, my coach, for your support and guidance over many years. Thank you, Colleen Henderson, for teaching me how to tell my story. Thank you colleagues and clients who agreed to be interviewed for this book. And thank you to all my clients who have courageously invited me into their organizations and their working lives, and invited me to accompany them on their journey through the world of work.

Another special thanks goes to my social media connections and my subscribers at WorkFeelsGood.com for sharing my updates and articles, and for your thoughtful and generous comments and support.

Lastly, thank you to all those who know me best and want the best for me: my friends, parents, and, most of all, my wife, Joanna.

Appendix
Your Team's Best Work

I N CHAPTER I, I mentioned that, during my transition from my corporate career to my consulting and coaching career, my appreciation of an authentic, responsible, and intentional relationship with work enabled me to be a better leader. As I began to understand how we make work meaningful, I was better able to engage my teams in their work. At that time, I began to notice how the best leaders were already engaging their teams in much the same way that I had become involved in succeeding at my authentic work.

When you're acting intentionally in the responsible pursuit of your authentic work, you are fully engaged in your work. Creating that same engagement in your team is actually easier than what you've already done for yourself, but there is one difference: You don't need to help your team members discover their authentic work. Instead, you only need to help them associate the work tasks they do with the contribution those tasks make to the well-being of others. As I discussed in Chapter 3, understanding how your work contributes to well-being is your greatest motivation to succeed. Similarly, the work done by an organization has the potential to contribute to the well-being of its customers and clients, the communities in which it operates, and all its employees. But these contributions are only possible when employees succeed at their work tasks. When I'm speaking to audiences or working with my clients, I use the diagram below to show the importance of associating tasks with contribution.

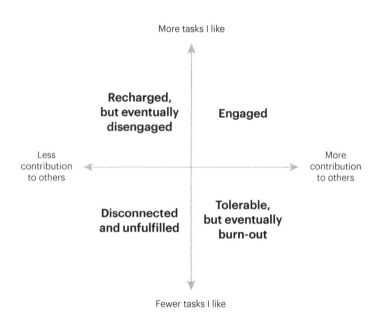

If your team members are doing work tasks they dislike, and if they cannot see how those tasks contribute to the well-being of others (lower-left quadrant), they'll soon feel unfulfilled and disconnected at work. But they will tolerate doing those tasks, for a part of their day or week, if they can see how they are contributing to others (lower-right quadrant). Of course, if they're always doing tasks they dislike only to contribute to the well-being of others, they will burn out.

Occasionally enabling team members to spend a little time on tasks they really enjoy but that don't substantially contribute to the well-being of others (upper-left quadrant) permits them to relax and recharge. But without a focus on contributing to others, not only will your team become less valuable to the organization, they will eventually become disengaged. Remember that contributing to well-being is our greatest motivation to succeed. Your team members will perform best when they are able to do tasks they enjoy and also see how those tasks contribute to well-being (upper-right quadrant). Your team is most engaged and performs best when they're working in this quadrant.

Regardless of whether you're developing an organization-wide employee engagement initiative or you're trying to boost one team member's engagement, the process for associating task with contribution is the same:

1   Connect people with others in the organization and create community. By creating relationships with other teams, your team members will begin to appreciate the interconnected and interdependent nature of your organization.

Working across the organization in this way also breaks down any "silos" that may have formed.

2   Show each team member how your team's purpose contributes to the success of the rest of the organization. Clarifying your team's purpose allows each team member to make that purpose personally meaningful.

3   Show each team member how her or his entire role contributes to the success of the team and the well-being of each member. Outlining the importance of their role—the sum of all their tasks—creates more meaningful relationships between team members.

4   Help team members associate their work tasks with the quadrants on the diagram. Doing so will enable them to identify any tasks in the Disconnected and Unfulfilled quadrant.

5   Help team members minimize tasks in the Recharged but Eventually Disengaged quadrant, accept that they may have to do tasks in the Tolerable quadrant, and maximize tasks in the Engaged quadrant.

Research shows that higher engagement is correlated to higher performance. Not only are the best leaders skilled at engaging their team, they are also fully engaged in their own leadership role. Being a leader is their authentic work.

Notes

Lillian Gish epigraph: Karen Weekes, *Women Know Everything: 3241 Quips, Quotes, and Brilliant Remarks* (Philadelphia, PA: Quirk Books, 2007).

Chapter 1

the most severe battle... since the Korean War: Historica Canada, "The battle of the Medak Pocket," retrieved from thecanadianencyclopedia.ca/en/article/battle-of-medak-pocket/.

Chapter 2

David Blustein described three primary motivations for work: D.L. Blustein, *The Psychology of Working: A New Perspective for Career Development, Counseling, and Public Policy* (Mahwah, NJ: Lawrence Erlbaum Associates, 2006).

many people want a best friend at work: Gallup, "Item 10: I Have a Best Friend at Work" (May 26, 1999), retrieved from news.gallup.com/businessjournal/511/item-10-best-friend-work.aspx.

Sociality is... within those groups: Edward O. Wilson, *The Social Conquest of Earth* (New York: Liveright Publishing, 2012).

humans are unique... because we are cultural animals: S. Solomon, J. Greenberg, and T. Pyszczynski, "The Cultural Animal: Twenty Years of Terror Management Theory and Research," in J. Greenberg, S.L. Koole, and T. Pyszczynski, eds., *Handbook of Experimental Existential Psychology* (New York: Guilford Press, 2004), 13–34.

"Culture and history and religion...": Julian Jaynes, *The Origin of Consciousness in the Breakdown of the Bicameral Mind* (New York: Mariner Books, 2000), 9.

Humans began to create culture about 3 million years ago...: Michael D. Petraglia and Ravi Korisettar, eds., *Early Human Behaviour in Global Context: The Rise and Diversity of the Lower Palaeolithic Record* (London: Routledge, 2005).

"humans 'solved' the problems...": Solomon, Greenberg, and Pyszczynski, "The Cultural Animal," 18.

Research into terror management theory...: E. Harmon-Jones, L. Simon, J. Greenberg, T. Pyszczynski, S. Solomon, and H. McGregor, "Terror Management Theory and Self-Esteem: Evidence That Increased Self-Esteem Reduced Mortality Salience Effects," *Journal of Personality and Social Psychology* 72, no. 1 (1997): 24–36.

Gretchen Rubin quote: Xabier K. Fernao, *365 Women Quotes: Daily Empowerment Quotes to Gain More Self-Confidence, Become More Productive and Achieve Your Wildest Goals* (2019).

The potential for any world view...: J. Greenberg, T. Pyszczynski, and S. Solomon, "The Causes and Consequences of a Need for Self-Esteem: A Terror Management Theory," in R.F. Baumeister, ed., *Public Self and Private Self* (New York: Springer-Verlag, 1986), 189–212.

Becker's book The Denial of Death: Ernest Becker, *The Denial of Death* (1974; repr., New York: Free Press, 1997).

Brené Brown quote: Brené Brown, *The Gifts of Imperfection: Let Go of Who You Think You're Supposed to Be and Embrace Who You Are* (Centre City, MN: Hazelden Publishing, 2010).

Chapter 3

Belief in an all-knowing person or thing...: Irvin D. Yalom, *Existential Psychotherapy* (Jackson, TN: Perseus Book Group, 1980).

Meredith Monk quote: Dr. Kathleen Cannon, *She Said What? Quotable Women Talk about Leadership* (2012).

"It is care that makes human existence meaningful...": Martin Heidegger, *Being and Time* (1953; repr., Albany: State University of New York Press, 2010).

care in the face of meaninglessness is authenticity: Heidegger, *Being and Time*.

"Neurosis is suffering...": James Hollis, *The Middle Passage: From Misery to Meaning in Midlife* (Toronto: Inner City Books, 1993).

Ella Winter quote: Weekes, *Women Know Everything*.

Sam Keen cautioned...: Becker, *Denial of Death*.

James Hollis, a Jungian scholar: James Hollis, *Creating a Life* (Toronto: Inner City Books, 2001).

TGIF... hump day... Monday blues: TGIF stands for "Thank God It's Friday" and celebrates the end of the working week and the happiness of a work-free weekend. "Hump day" is a euphemism for Wednesday and celebrates getting to the middle of the workweek. "Monday blues" refers to unhappiness at having to start another week of work.

Chapter 4

On April 12, 2018...: Michelle Kim and Ben Fuerherd, "Starbucks Worker Hands Coffee, Pastries to Surprised NYPD, FDNY Personnel at Chelsea Blast Site," Channel 4 website (September 19, 2016), retrieved July 5, 2018, nbcnewyork.com/news/local/Starbucks-Employee-Gives-Cops-Coffee-at -Chelsea-Blast-Site-394037941.html.

Starbucks closed eight thousand...: Rachel Siegel, "Here's What to Expect from Today's Starbucks Racial Bias Training," *Washington Post*, May 29, 2018, washingtonpost.com/news/business/wp/2018/05/23/not-who-we-aspire-to -be-starbucks-previews-next-weeks-racial-bias-training-for-8000-employees /?noredirect=on&utm_term=.d95a2d4e974e.

After one explosion in Manhattan...: Kim and Fuerherd, "Starbucks Worker."

Werewere Liking quote: J. Stewart, *Stewart's Quotable African Women* (London: Penguin Group, 2005), Kindle.

Melissa believes that the world needs to reduce fossil fuel consumption: To learn how some leaders in the energy industry support the science of climate change, are committed to the responsible development of fossil fuels, and are committed to reducing their own carbon footprint, read what the CEO of Suncor said on June 6, 2018, at a conference titled "Bridging Divides: In Search of Sound Public Policies for Energy and Environment in Canada," at cbc.ca/ news/canada/calgary/suncor-ceo-slams-climate-change-deniers-1.4694549.

Jeff has always been committed...: The well-being of humanity depends on solving the social and environmental problems that threaten our world. Many people dedicated to solutions are working in the most responsible way. One example is the work of Bjorn Lomborg and the Copenhagen Consensus Center: "The Copenhagen Consensus Center is a think tank that researches the smartest solutions for the world's biggest problems, advising policy-makers and philanthropists how to spend their money most effectively" (copenhagenconsensus.com/our-story).

Dalene Matthee quote: Stewart, *Stewart's Quotable African Women.*

Research shows that humans are more likely to be good...: One of the dominant themes in evolutionary psychology is that co-operation and kindness are naturally selected. See also Keltner's *Born to Be Good* (cited below).

Evolutionary scientists can show...: L.A. Penner, J.F. Dovidio, J.A. Piliavin, and D.A. Schroeder, "Prosocial Behavior: Multilevel Perspectives," *Annual Review of Psychology* 56 (2005): 365-92.

Studies have shown that reminders of our own death...: E. Jonas, J. Schimel, J. Greenberg, and T. Pyszczynski, "The Scrooge Effect: Evidence That Mortality Salience Increases Prosocial Attitudes and Behavior," *Personality and Social Psychology Bulletin* 28, no. 10 (2002): 1342-53.

... *the feel-good chemical dopamine*: Dacher Keltner, *Born to Be Good: The Science of a Meaningful Life* (New York: W.W. Norton, 2009).

Elizabeth Cady Stanton quote: Peggy Anderson, *Great Quotes from Great Women* (Franklin Lakes, NJ: Career Press, 1997).

Charlotte Perkins Gilman quote: Cannon, *She Said What?*

In his bestselling book Start with Why: Simon Sinek, *Start with Why: How Great Leaders Inspire Everyone to Take Action* (London: Penguin Books, 2009).

Chapter 5

George B. Leonard quote: G.B. Leonard, *The Ultimate Athlete* (Berkeley, CA: North Atlantic Books, 1987).

In recent years, physicists have advanced theories... see the relational interpretation of quantum mechanics https://en.wikipedia.org/wiki/Relational _quantum_mechanics

Audre Lorde quote: Audrey Lorde, *The Cancer Journals*, Special Edition (San Francisco: Aunt Lute Books, 1997).

... *your goals should be SMART*: George T. Doran first proposed SMART goals in the 1981 issue of *Management Review.*

Madonna quote: Cannon, *She Said What?*

Dorothy Height quote: Ibid.

Robyn Davidson quote: Ibid.

Conclusion

Amelia Earhart quote: W.A. Albion, *The Quotable Amelia Earhart* (Albuquerque: University of New Mexico Press, 2015).

About the Author

TOM MORIN IS an inspiring speaker and writer who is redefining meaningful work and leadership development. Tom's challenging and sometimes dangerous working life has inspired his mission to create a better world of work for ourselves and future generations.

After his military career, Tom became a project manager and people leader in multinational corporations. Toward the end of his corporate career, he co-founded Work Innovation Partners before providing consulting and coaching services through Work Feels Good. Tom has completed graduate studies in the social sciences and researched various topics in leadership and organizational behaviour. He is Associate Faculty at Royal Roads University, where he was a recipient of the University Founders' Award, and an instructor at Mount Royal University. Tom's consulting and coaching practice is focused on leadership in critical moments and helping individuals and organizations make work meaningful.

To learn more about Tom Morin, go to WorkFeelsGood.com.

CPSIA information can be obtained
at www.ICGtesting.com
Printed in the USA
LVHW110721160220
647042LV00004B/4